LIGHT
BELONGS
IN
THE
DARKNESS

PATRICIA KING

LIGHT
BELONGS
IN
THE
DARKNESS

*FINDING YOUR PLACE IN
GOD'S ENDTIME HARVEST*

Destiny Image® Publishers, Inc.

P.O. Box 310

Shippensburg, PA 17257-0310

"Speaking to the Purposes of God for
This Generation and for the Generations to Come"

ISBN 0-7684-2291-4

For Worldwide Distribution
Printed in the U.S.A.

This book and all other Destiny Image, Revival Press, MercyPlace, Fresh Bread, Destiny Image Fiction, and Treasure House books are available at Christian bookstores and distributors worldwide.

2 3 4 5 6 7 8 9 10 / 10 09 08 07 06 05

Call toll-free
1-800-722-6774.

For more information on foreign distributors, call
717-532-3040.

Or reach us on the Internet:
www.destinyimage.com

Dedicated To

TODD BENTLEY,

whose passion for the gospel
has ignited my heart with fresh fire.

STACEY CAMPBELL,

whose prophetic words have rocked my world.

HEIDI AND ROLLAND BAKER,

whose light shines constantly in the darkness
and makes me want more of Jesus.

STEVE COURT AND DANIELLE STRICKLAND,

who have challenged my walk
through their example of doing the stuff!

Special Thanks To

The staff and team at Extreme Prophetic.

All our partners and intercessors.

Thanks for being committed to taking
the light into the darkness!

Endorsements

"I had to read over fifty books on evangelism for my doctoral dissertation while I was at Fuller Seminary. I wish Patricia's new book, *Light Belongs in the Darkness*, was out then because it is one of the best books I have read on evangelism. I believe that this book will equip, inspire and impart a fresh anointing for evangelism and will be a major catalyst for fulfilling the Great Commission."

Dr. Che Ahn
Sr. Pastor
Harvest Rock Church

"*Light Belongs in the Darkness* is lethal! It will jolt you free from lethargic churchianity and energize you towards relevant Christianity. Receive a fresh encounter with the Holy Spirit as you read this timely book by my friend Patricia King. The message and the messenger have become one in this radical call to prophetic evangelism!"

James W. Goll
Cofounder of Encounters Network
Author of, *The Seer* and *The Lost Art of Intercession*

"Connecting powerful prophetic ministry with the desperate needs of humanity is a must for today's Church. In a culture often describing itself as post-Christian, the shock of God's powerful yet loving intervention is what is needed for many to accept Christ. This book will show you what prophetic evangelism looks like and how you can operate it."

John Arnott
Senior Pastor
Toronto Airport Christian Fellowship

"Patricia King doesn't just teach and preach this stuff. She lives it. In the streets. So many believers today ask, "Where is the Church heading? And what will it look like?" Patricia King is leading the way. The Church is about to be seen again—where Jesus was seen—with those who are lost, sick, and dying. In other words, Jesus did His work "in the world"—the world He created. In the same way, the Church—that is, believers—are about to relocate themselves "into the world." If you don't believe me, read Patricia's book, *Light Belongs in the Darkness*."

Steve Shultz,
THE ELIJAH LIST

"The Kingdom of God invades the kingdom of darkness with this revelatory book that reveals the power of the prophetic as an evangelistic tool. Patricia King's book, *Light Belongs in the Darkness*, is a must read for every Christian seeking to follow Jesus' command to preach the Gospel. King pulls back the veil on many common myths, fearlessly confronts controversial questions shrouding the prophetic, and gives practical applications and life changing examples for every believer. Readers are empowered with fresh creativity and vision for the end times' Church and God's urgent calling for today's harvest."

Jill Austin,
Master Potter Ministries
www.masterpotter.com

"Patricia King's new book, *Light Belongs in the Darkness*, is an inspiring call to action, filled with powerful stories of how to confront darkness in the marketplace. This 'how to' book will challenge and equip God's people to rise up in the spirit of Elijah to decree and demonstrate our God as a God of Power. I truly recommend this book for those who desire to become a burning and shining lamp that will ignite revival fires."

Todd Bentley
Evangelist, Fresh Fire Ministries

Table of Contents

Foreword

Many books are written about what *could* or *should be*. They are filled with ideas and theories—all of which are built on the principles of Scripture or the implied possibilities found in the history of the Church. Dreamers usually write them. They have their place because they help us to think differently, and they inspire us to dream. But they usually fall short of their potential in that they can't provide a model to follow, and often die in the classroom.

Light Belongs in the Darkness is not such a book. Although it will cause you to think differently and will definitely give birth to new dreams, it is not a book of theories. It is a record of what is quickly becoming a new norm for Christians around the world.

One of the greatest compliments I can give a person is that "they are what they teach." Patricia King lived this book long before she wrote it. The impact of her life is stunning and will now reach far beyond her ability to travel.

I got excited reading this book! First of all, because I love the truth she proclaims. The stories provoked me to pursue

Him more. The risks I've been taking are good, but there is so much more! She sets a godly pace. Secondly, it was because I could see the vast numbers of people that would be impacted by these truths. As I travel, I become overwhelmed by the incredible hunger in the Body of Christ. People want the authentic and will pay any price to get it. Patricia brings that message—she is that message. This book must be read by anyone who burns with the conviction that there is more, and they won't settle for yesterday's norm.

There is a passionate generation arising that will not settle for concepts, ideas, and theories. They insist on the gospel of the Scriptures—one that is experienced, and knows no impossibilities. It must be practical, powerful, and doable. This book was written in response to their cries.

Bill Johnson
Senior Pastor, Bethel Church; Redding, California
Author of *When Heaven Invades Earth*
and *The Supernatural Power of a Transformed Mind*

1

CHAPTER

Power in the Streets

...BUT YOU WILL RECEIVE POWER WHEN THE
HOLY SPIRIT COMES ON YOU; AND YOU WILL BE
MY WITNESSES...(ACTS 1:8).

Following Christ's ascension, the disciples went to Jerusalem and stationed themselves in the upper room for a continual devotion to prayer. With undivided focus, they locked into a vision planted in their hearts through words spoken to them by Jesus.

I am going to send you what My Father has promised; but stay in the city until you have been clothed with power from on high (Luke 24:49).

But you will receive power when the Holy Spirit comes on you; and you will be My witnesses in Jerusalem, and in all Judea and Samaria, and to the ends of the earth (Acts 1:8).

The disciples were preparing to receive power. But this power would not make their life easier or grant them a favored reputation. They understood the responsibility of such power as they had observed their Lord walk in it. The disciples also understood the persecution brought about by such power as they had personally encountered it.

As they proclaimed Jesus as Messiah into the uttermost parts of the earth, this power would prepare them for persecution and resistance. When demonstrated, this power would fill the earth with knowledge of the Lord's glory. Supernatural power from on high could not be denied once someone had been touched by it. But now, the disciples were going to be fully clothed with this power. The fullness of the grace and anointing that they had seen Christ walk in was now to come upon them.

Those days in the upper room were set apart as a consecration period. During this time, the cost of serving Christ was weighed. The disciples spent time to lay down any personal agendas. They knew that their walk wouldn't be as it had been before, but how would it be? Jesus had taught them about a new wineskin, but what would that look like?

I am sure they reviewed all the words Christ taught them, such as: "…anyone who has faith in Me will do what I have been doing. He will do even greater things than these, because I am going to the Father" (John 14:12) and "As the Father has sent Me, I am sending you" (John 20:21). How exciting this time must have been! Faith must have risen in their hearts as they meditated on these promises. Certainly, fresh vision entered as the disciples saw themselves in the light of Christ's proclaimed potential. They were called to carry light into the darkness.

At that time, political and economical circumstances made it difficult for Jewish people. This wasn't an easy hour to proclaim Christ. Many religious leaders were irate, others were confused about Christ's death, and some were skeptical regarding the alleged resurrection. No wonder the disciples needed a power that would enable them to live for the gospel and to die for it as well as. This power would allow them to leave all for His sake; they needed this divine, raw power. The group of men and women in the upper room were completely abandoned to God's purposes and cared nothing for their own lives and reputations. Whatever the cost, they had a passion to see Christ's gospel made known and to advance the Kingdom of God.

To follow Jesus they left employment positions as fishermen, tax collectors, and physicians. Imagine what their families must have thought when they left stable, and perhaps even lucrative, careers to follow a preacher. Jesus wasn't the most popular person among the Jews, but He was the most controversial. So, the disciples made a decision to follow Him, after which they experienced miracles, signs, and wonders as well as ridicule, slander, and opposition.

After only three years of the disciples' following Jesus, He was arrested for blasphemy. His disciples must have expected a miracle of deliverance and vindication to prove His deity. But, instead, He was tried, convicted, and hung. The masses witnessed His death on the Cross. He was finished, or so they thought. Can you imagine being one of Christ's disciples on that day? What would you tell family and friends who had all along criticized you for following this man? During this time, I am sure the disciples felt very vulnerable and, even possibly, struggled with their commitment to the gospel. Was the message for real? Should they return to fishing? Perhaps all their relatives and friends were right, and they never should have left everything to follow this preacher. But what about all the promises He spoke of?

Christ, however, *was* raised from the dead and appeared to His disciples and some others. But not everyone in the region saw Him, so not everyone believed reports of His resurrection. In fact, even the disciples needed time to receive an assurance of their faith. Thomas, who was the ultimate doubter, said he would not believe in the resurrection until he could actually feel the holes in His hands and side.

Jesus' appearance must have deeply encouraged the disciples' faith. However, He didn't remain long with them. Over the 40 days following His resurrection, Jesus taught them many lessons, and then commissioned them to spread the gospel into the entire world. He explained carefully that they needed the Holy Spirit's power to fulfill this awesome mandate.

Then, He left. That's right, He exited the scene. The disciples were left all alone to wait for the promised Spirit. In obedience to Christ, they went to Jerusalem and waited in the upper room to be visited by power from on high. What should they expect from this promise? Jesus didn't explain what the empowerment would feel like or how it would arrive. The disciples waited together and prayed continuously in one accord. One day, two days, and then three days passed, yet they were still praying and waiting. I wonder if they doubted whether they had heard Jesus accurately. Four days, five days, and then six days went by, but still no Holy Spirit power. Seven days, eight days, and nine days came and went, but they still had no visitation.

Maybe they questioned how they were going to pay their bills. After all, who would support them? The disciples may have thought, *"It's been nine days. Maybe we should go and get some work. How are we going to eat? We've been hanging out here for nine days already and no visitation yet. Perhaps we didn't hear right."* Most of the population believed Jesus to be a false prophet and were not impressed with the disciples' faith. Also, it wasn't like their appointment calendars were filled with speaking engagements. I am sure they didn't have a large partner base, if any at all. How would they pay the bill on the room they were waiting in? It had been nine days and still no Holy Spirit.

Finally, the moment happened. The noise of a rushing wind brought a violent, tangible manifestation, and the whole house was filled with the Spirit's presence. The appearance of tongues of fire rested on each disciple and everyone began to speak in unlearned languages. The Spirit came so dramatically that the disciples appeared drunk on sweet wine. When the sound occurred, a crowd gathered in amazement and perplexity. How awesome! Peter stood up and spoke with boldness as he testified of the Christ. Conviction of the reality of a resurrected Christ fell on the streets and impacted the masses. Three thousand people called on the name of the Lord that day and were saved. Through the apostles' ministry, miracles, signs, and wonders broke out on the streets and more souls joined the Kingdom. The Holy Spirit came into the upper room, and then flooded the streets to birth the Church with a tangible demonstration of power.

But persecution began immediately, and resistance to the gospel rose up in strength. As the opposition began, however, Christ's power simply increased all the more. The Kingdom's advancing was unstoppable, even amidst riots, slander, public trials, stonings, and jail sentences. The gospel spread into the world like wildfire. Jesus had taught that the gates of hell would not prevail as the disciples moved forward with the revelation of Christ. Now, they were seeing the living evidence of that word.

The power that visited the disciples in the upper room enabled them to stand firm amidst all the turmoil. The early Church emerged through an abandoned group of men and women who cared nothing for their own lives and reputations. Now clothed with power from on high, they became enabled to live and die for the gospel. What consumed them was a passion to be sent as Christ's witnesses into the furthest parts of the earth.

WHAT IS NORMAL?

During that perplexing outpouring of the Spirit's power on the Day of Pentecost, Peter stood up among the masses and declared:

> ...this is what was spoken by the prophet Joel: "In the last days, God says, I will pour out My Spirit on all people. Your sons and your daughters will prophesy, your young men will see visions, your old men will dream dreams. Even on My servants, both men and women, I will pour out My Spirit in those days and they will prophesy. I will show wonders in the heaven above and signs in the earth below..." (Acts 2:16-19).

The Spirit's power birthed the Church in the streets, and Peter declared a prophecy of the last days: The Lord's servants would speak and act on God's behalf, signs and wonders would be performed, and God's Spirit would be poured out on all people. In verse 21 of that same passage, Peter decreed, "And everyone who calls on the name of the Lord will be saved."

The power explosion seen on the streets during the Day of Pentecost is the prototype for the emerging, last-days Church. Throughout the Book of Acts, God's Kingdom truly manifested in power through His servants. Sick people were healed, demons were cast out, the dead were raised, angelic visitations were common, and supernatural occurrences regularly confirmed Christ's authority in the earth. All of this is actually what the Church is supposed to look like.

Souls were saved everywhere the apostles preached the gospel. The Kingdom advanced with demonstrations of power in their ministry, just as Jesus proclaimed. He had commissioned the disciples to preach the gospel of the Kingdom with power: "The kingdom of heaven is near. Heal the sick, raise the dead, cleanse those who have leprosy, drive out demons"

(Matt. 10:8). Such miraculous ministry should be the norm for Kingdom advancement in the earth.

A New Wave of Power

We are on the verge of a new outpouring of the Spirit that will not be found inside of church buildings as much as it will be evidenced amongst the lost. The apostolic Church—which is commissioned to preach the gospel and perform Kingdom wonders—is arising in the earth right now. Many nations are already showing an amazing advancement of the Kingdom.

Some time ago, I was watching some video footage of an apostolic minister in Africa. In the name of Jesus, He prayed for a woman with lip cancer to be healed; He didn't lay hands on her, but simply gave the faith command. Within moments, the cancer began to leave her body, and an ugly, thick, slimy substance poured out of her lips. Hours later, the cancer was completely gone and within days her lips had totally returned to normal. The film footage that showed her before and after the miracle was astounding. After that, the woman received healing from cancer within her internal organs.

Todd Bentley, a young evangelist, is a great personal friend of mine. Within a few short years, he has won hundreds of thousands of people to the Lord. He lives on the radical edge of a tenacious faith. While preaching in Africa once, he hit strong resistance from the Moslem population, which threatened his life. The next day, Todd took his team to the local fish market where he preached from a box. He boldly invited people there to come forward to receive a miracle. In fact, Todd was so filled with courage by the Spirit that he promised that if they did not receive a miracle, then he would go home and deny the Bible as being true. That piqued everyone's curiosity and a number of people took up his challenge. Right there in public, each one was gloriously healed through a miracle of the Spirit. As a result of this power confrontation, many more came forward for healing and deliverance. That afternoon, Todd's entire team was kept busy and led numerous Moslems to Christ.

One minister in Mexico, David Hogan, preaches the good news with his team to unreached villages on a continual basis. The sick are healed, demons are cast out, and hundreds have been raised from the dead. Reports from China, India, and South America also confirm supernatural accounts of Kingdom power accompanied by a harvest of souls. These events are normal Christianity and are happening right now. In the 21st century, the gospel is spreading in the same manner that Jesus said it would.

This wave of gospel power is also going to reach the Western world. It must! As God's people lay hold of the promises, a revival is going to hit the streets with great impact. Prophetic gifts, healings, and miracles taken to the streets are being confirmed by God with signs that follow. As we go in Christ's name to the afflicted, these gifts will flow naturally. All of us are not necessarily called to the spectacular, but we are all called to walk in the supernatural. When we are relaxed and free to be ourselves, that is when the supernatural flows, and it's not always in a flashy, loud, or demonstrative way. After all, it is Christ *in us* that is the hope of glory.

A New Adam in Just Five Hours

I met Adam during a School of Extreme Prophetic summer outreach in inner-city Vancouver. He was 23 years old and an addict infected with Hepatitis C. A young prophetic evangelist, Faytene Kryskow, brought him to Stacey Campbell and I for a prophetic blessing. Faytene had been sharing the gospel with Adam but wanted us to minister a special prophetic word over his life. We prayed and brought some encouraging prophecies that awakened him somewhat to the reality of God. Although touched by the words, Adam was still not convinced that Jesus Christ was Lord. As Adam wrestled through a number of issues, he questioned us about the options of other religions and spiritual powers. Suddenly, a word of knowledge rose up in me and I boldly declared: "Within the next 48 hours, Jesus Christ is going to confirm to you in a tangible way that He is God." Adam looked rather shocked at the strong statement and shrugged his shoulders. I repeated, "Within 48 hours, Jesus will give you tangible proof." He said, "I'll believe it when I see it."

After this prophetic encounter, I left with our team for dinner. Following our meal and fellowship, we once again hit the streets and, this time, visited our "prophetic massage" team. Many drug addicts suffer with sore muscles, so we offered them a free shoulder massage while we prayed and prophesied destiny over their lives. Massage chairs were all lined up on the street, with traffic going by and pedestrians passing through. Every chair was filled with those hungry to receive this inspired "laying on of hands" ministry. Standing right across from the massage chairs, we saw Adam, grinning from ear to ear. He looked at me with excitement and loudly proclaimed, "It's only been 5 hours!" He repeated, "It's only been 5 hours! You said that Jesus would confirm Himself to me within 48 hours, but it's only been 5 hours."

Adam explained that the day before we met him, he had fallen off his bike and badly wounded his shoulder and back. One of the outreach team members prayed for healing, and Adam experienced a miracle: all the pain completely left his body and he regained total mobility before the prayer was even finished. After Adam finished recounting his miracle, I asked, "So do you believe now that Jesus is Lord?" He answered unashamedly, "Oh yeah! You guys have made a believer out of me!" Then I said, "Would you like to surrender your life to Him now?" Adam replied, "You bet!"

So, Adam became a new creation in Christ. Joy filled his entire being. He also received prayer for deliverance from addiction and healing for hepatitis. This moment marked the beginning of the rest of his life. When Adam attended our meetings the next day, he sat in the front row and was still beaming. During the night, the Lord had visited him with more confirmations and Adam was overflowing with gratefulness. Less than 24 hours saved, Adam stood up before an audience of about 100 people. Delivered from pain and addiction, he boldly testified of His salvation experience.

The believers who live and minister in the inner city embraced him, and immediately Adam became aware of a whole new family. He followed up his salvation by getting involved with a ministry group. Many times he has shared his testimony, punctuated with favorite phrases like, "I just love the Big Guy," and, "I thank God every day. I thank Him so much!" Adam is now on the streets, where he shares the gospel and is being powerfully used by the Lord.

FREEDOM TO PRISONERS

The streets are full of lonely, confused people awaiting a power encounter of God for their lives. During an outreach in Las Vegas, our prophetic teams met a man who had just been released from prison that very day. After having been sentenced to a 20-year prison term, he got released after 13 years. Lost and very alone, he was frightened for his future and unsure of how to fit into society.

Stacey Campbell prophesied words of hope and destiny over his life. She also received words of knowledge concerning what happened to him as a little boy. The power of God's love touched his heart and he wept as the prophetic ministry continued. Following the prayer, the man shared that he had never felt such love in his entire life. God's supernatural love power penetrated his heart and he immediately gave his life to Jesus

Christ. In 13 minutes of prophetic ministry on the street, the Lord achieved more for this man than his professional counselors did during 13 years of therapy sessions. This is the power of God. This is the Kingdom!

On other occasions we visited prisons. During one trip to an institution for juvenile offenders, we found the young men extremely spiritually hungry and eager for a touch by the Lord's presence. After prophesying over a couple of residents, numerous others lined up for prophetic words: they wanted a power encounter. That day, each one received a prophetic word of encouragement. Some fell down under the power of the Spirit, a few wept uncontrollably, and others received physical and emotional healing. Many felt the tangible presence of God's love and peace on their lives, while a few laughed uncontrollably as they experienced a deep inner release in the fullness of joy.

GOD ENCOUNTERS ON THE STREET

One "God encounter" can change a person's life forever. Erica Greve is a passionate believer who did an internship with us during her third year of Bible school. While walking through Vancouver's inner city, she met a fellow who was smoking some crack cocaine right in public view. Erica stopped and stood in front of him, noticing that the side of his head was seriously scarred from a previous injury. The man explained that, years previously, someone had jammed an ice pick through his ear. As a result, he had lost hearing in one ear and also suffered constant, severe head pain. He agreed to have Erica pray for him, which she did immediately. The power of God touched him miraculously, and he suddenly could hear clearly out of the damaged ear, and all his head pain vanished. God is not a respecter of persons. He longs to demonstrate His "love power" through any willing vessel.

During that same school, one of our teams advertised prayer by wearing a sandwich board that read: *"Got Hep C? Need a Miracle? FREE PRAYER."* At that time, over 90 percent of injectable drug users in the inner city of Vancouver were infected with Hepatitis C. This serious epidemic needed the intervention of God. Our team wore their sandwich boards while walking in Pigeon Park, which is an area populated by many drug addicts. Individuals saw the message on the sandwich board and asked for prayer. One man got so blasted by the power of God that he crashed to the ground and was unable to stand up as the Lord's healing touch rushed through his body. Other people said that they felt heat go right through them.

While on a street in Los Angeles, Erica and Shirley Ross (producer of our *Extreme Prophetic* television program) met a man who could hardly walk straight due to intoxication. The obviously disorientated man was also badly burned from over-exposure to the sun. Erica asked the man if he needed some help. He looked a bit puzzled and couldn't answer very clearly, but he managed to nod his head in the affirmative. After unsuccessful attempts at communicating through his drug stupor, Erica commanded him to sober up in the name of Jesus. Immediately, his head jolted back and then flopped forward; he miraculously became coherent and able to communicate. In the midst of an L.A. street, the man stood absolutely amazed at the touch of God's power, and then gave his life to Jesus. Shirley happened to have the television camera with her and filmed the entire process. Before your very eyes, you can actually see God's deliverance power touch his life. The transformation of his countenance was very visible, as was his behavior. Yet another soul was reached for the Lord.

WHAT ABOUT YOU?

These testimonies did not take place in a church building, but on city streets. These miracles were worked through ordinary people who became available vessels filled with God's power and presence. They were willing to go to the streets to seek those who were lost. What about you? Are you willing to go? If so, then the Holy Spirit is both willing and able to fill you with the same power and anointing received by members of the early Church on the Day of Pentecost. Perhaps, like the disciples in the Book of Acts who waited for the promise of power, we also need to find our upper room. Perhaps, like them, we also need to determine our passion and the willingness to live and die for Christ.

2
CHAPTER

Run with the Vision

IN HIM WAS LIFE, AND THAT LIFE WAS THE
LIGHT OF MEN. THE LIGHT SHINES IN THE
DARKNESS, BUT THE DARKNESS HAS NOT OVER-
POWERED IT (JOHN 1:4-5).

The torch bearer sheepishly ascended the golden stairway that led to the massive altar. Trembling in absolute awe of the consuming fire that blazed ahead, she extended an unlit baton into the inferno. Drawing it out after a number of moments, she beheld the torch in amazement, as it now illuminated with an indescribable, unquenchable fire. Looking away from the torch to gaze once more at the altar, she stood speechless and oh so still. The atmosphere was silent—almost too much so. Then, an audible voice—not just a voice, but *the Voice*—shook the environment around her and commanded with unquestionable authority, *"Run with the vision, run with the vision, run with the vision."*

The runner was to race with the torch held high. She was convinced that her mandate was not about her, but about the eternal light she carried. In response to the divine command that continued to echo vehemently within her heart, she ran down the stairs with strength and purpose, with the torch raised high. As she raced swiftly into a path saturated in deep darkness, she found her pace accelerating. Her feet were seemingly bound to an ordained roadway. A powerful presence of supernatural grace propelled her along the route. Her focus was undisturbed. She experienced a sense of weightlessness and inner rest as her body vigorously ran through darkness toward an unknown destination. No sign of fatigue or weariness bore upon her, only the essence of exhilaration. Her mission was clear and simple: Hold the torch high and run with the vision.

On each side of the path, eyes peered through the darkness. Although the runner was aware of her unseen observers, she was neither impressed nor distracted. Her mandate completely consumed her attention and focus. She continued to run for a fair distance when, in the distance, the heavens all of a sudden rolled back to fill the horizon with brilliant flashes of light blue sky and glistening white clouds. Instead of running into darkness, she was now racing into heavenly glory. The path of pure transparent gold was now in clear view. As she ascended the path into the heavenlies, the runner continued with fervency in stride.

A loud chorus of celestial voices cheered and shouted. "Here they come! Here they come!" The runner was puzzled and thought, *Here they come? Who are they?* Taking a moment to glance behind, she was shocked to see a multitude of people from every nation running on the golden pathway. Everywhere the torch had gone had brought illumination and brilliance; there was no darkness. Multitudes now followed in this radiant light along a golden roadway into life everlasting. Heaven was cheering and celebrating with an indescribable excitement.

That was the end of a vision I encountered in August 1980, but not the end of the experience. In this divine encounter, I was under the power of the Spirit and every cell in my body shook with the power of joy. I felt every organ and every cell within me vibrate with pleasure. I lay there laughing uncontrollably for what seemed like a long time. In the presence of the Lord, there is fullness of joy! (See Psalm 16:11).

This vision is a prophetic word concerning the hour we are now living in. The runner represents the last-day Church. The prophet Isaiah foretold of a time amid dark, evil days when believers would reveal the Lord's light of glory and people would see it and follow.

> *Arise, shine for your light has come, and the glory of the Lord rises upon you. See, darkness covers the earth and thick darkness is over the peoples, but the Lord rises upon you and His glory appears over you. Nations will come to your light, and kings to the brightness of your dawn* (Isaiah 60:1-3).

The true believer will shine brightly amidst an atmosphere of moral decay, idolatry, lawlessness, immorality, terrorism, and rebellion.

A RADICAL COMPANY

At this time, a radical company of Christians is being raised up by the Lord. Not interested in its own agenda, reputation, or platform, this company is called to one mandate: to lift up the exalted Christ in the earth. Special grace will be granted to torch bearers who run with pure focus in an unwavering commitment to Kingdom advancement. Through miracles, signs, and wonders, they will lift up the light of the Lord. They will speak authoritative prophetic decrees of God's purposes, just as Elijah did as he stood before the prophets of Baal. They will let their light shine before men as they manifest works of the Kingdom. They will be known for love, goodness, and compassion. Many names will be unrecognizable to the masses for they are not looking for fame; they understand what it means to be hidden in Christ. Others will be brought out of obscurity so that their names are well-known; but these will understand the cost of such responsibility and make sure to guard their hearts.

This special company of consecrated vessels will see multitudes come to the Lord. Who is this company? Does it only consist of a few? How are they chosen? Are they only the uniquely gifted? Matthew 9:35-36 shows Jesus preaching the gospel throughout villages and cities while healing every kind of sickness and disease. He looked upon the masses with compassion because they were downcast, like sheep without a shepherd. In Matthew 9:36-37, He said to the disciples, "The harvest is plentiful but the workers are few. Ask the Lord of the harvest, therefore, to send out workers into His harvest field."

The Lord is searching for those willing to carry the torch. He wants those without compromise who will exalt His name and let His light shine. He is looking for those willing to run with the vision of the gospel of the Kingdom. He yearns for those who will yield to Him and accept the grace that awaits anyone who says, "Yes." Who is called to this company? Anyone who is willing; you are called and I am called. Right now, the harvest is waiting to be plucked. Jesus said, "Do you not say, 'Four months more and then the harvest?' I tell you, open your eyes and look at the fields! They are ripe for harvest" (John 4:35). A key phrase in this passage is "open your eyes and look at the fields." If you look for lost souls, you will find them. If you look for doors to preach the gospel through, you will see them open.

Todd Bentley has won hundreds of thousands of people to Christ in just a few years. He simply lifted up his eyes to see the ripened harvest fields of the earth. He trusted God to empower him to do the work of the gospel, and the Lord blessed him with an international signs and wonders ministry that is lead-ing masses of people to Christ. Many other firebrands for the Lord are bringing in the sheaves with joy simply because they see the harvest and go after it. Lift up your eyes. Look at your neighborhood, your workplace, your family. Lift up your eyes and see the lonely, the afflicted, the hurting, and the lost. They are all around you. We are in a harvest season now. Are you ready to be recruited? Are you ready to *run with the vision?* The harvest awaits you!

DISCERNING THE TIMES AND SEASONS

It is always the right time to bring a soul to Christ. Every day, there is potential to reach someone who is ready to be "harvested." There are, however, particular seasons in the earth for a mass move of evangelism; these are God-appointed times for God-appointed assignments. During these seasons, special grace is given to fulfill His mandate for harvesting souls into the Kingdom. Both the assignment and its timing need to be discerned. Then, the Church must be quickly mobilized. Most often, prophets assist the Body of Christ in discerning the times and then inform them on how to engage in the season. (Apostles then build strategies for mobilization. Evangelists equip believers to reach the lost. Pastors and teachers prepare the Church for discipleship duties.)

Four seasons exist in the natural cycle of life. In fall, farm-ers collect seed from the crops. This seed will then be planted in the following spring. If the farmer does not move quickly to harvest the seed, then he will not have any for the next year. Harvesting seed is a specific function that must be done in the right season. All farmers understand this, so diligent farmers harvest seeds in the fall, which is God's appointed time for seed harvesting. A wise farmer will not miss the God-appointed time for a God-appointed task.

When winter comes, everything is at rest. Nothing grows in the cold of winter as it is not a season for growth. Winter is a season for rest so that renewal can follow a few months later. If you attempt to either plant or harvest in winter, you will be extremely disappointed. It is not a God-appointed time for harvest, but is a God-appointed season for rest.

Then comes spring, which is a season to sow seed. If you don't sow in this season, you will miss the harvest that follows. You don't sow in the fall, winter, or summer, but in the spring. Farmers discern the season and, in wisdom, plant seed with an expectation of a harvest.

Finally, summer arrives, which allows the seeds planted in spring to quickly grow under warm sunshine and refreshing rains. During the summer season, fruit is produced and crop harvesting begins. Mid-to-late summer and early fall are typical seasons of harvest. Ripened fields are ready to reap overnight, and the farmer must immediately bring in matured fields of produce, fruit, and grain. When time comes to reap a specific crop, you must harvest or else lose the yield. Crops do not wait until farmers are ready, so farmers must be ready to go as soon as the crop is ripe.

Early in our marriage, my husband Ron and I lived on a farm. The summer crops were ready at various times. Some vegetables matured early and others later, but they became ready whether we were or not. One crop we harvested was alfalfa. The animals ate the alfalfa over the winter, so having a large supply stored up in the barn was critical. Each day during harvest season, the farmer would carefully watch both the ripening field and the weather. One day, he ran over to our home and said, "We need to go *now!* A storm is forecasted for tomorrow and we need to get the crop in *today!*" So we rolled up our sleeves and went to work. We worked day and night, because if we didn't get the harvest in immediately, we would lose it.

This natural example reveals a picture of spiritual seasons. In the corporate Body of Christ, there are seasons for rest, sowing, harvesting seeds, and harvesting the fruit of our labors. For the Western Church, the 1990s was a decade of renewal and not harvest, even though, as I said earlier, there is always an opportunity to lead a soul to Christ. Massive harvests were taking place in Africa, South America, and other places in the '90s, but not so much in the Western world. Each crop has a specific season for harvest, and for Western nations that time is at hand.

God's focus in the West has been more on the Church, although we did receive little foretastes of harvest during the 1990s (like the Brownsville Revival of Pensacola, Florida). Beginning in 1994, the Lord visited believers all over the world with a Spirit outpouring launched globally through the Father's Blessing at the Toronto Airport Christian Fellowship in Canada. In corporate gatherings, His manifest presence was so heavy that many people staggered about in drunken stupors while "under the influence" of the Holy Spirit.

During that decade, the Church was filled with new fire and excitement. People flocked to Christian conferences and gatherings by the thousands. If you missed jumping into the river during that season, you missed it! I'm not saying that the river of living water isn't flowing from the throne each day for every believer. God will always bless His people, and His covenant promises are for all times. But those years had an outpouring designed by God to touch His corporate Body. During that season, His manifest presence was definitely found in the midst of gathered believers.

We are in a different season now. In Song of Solomon 3, we find the Shulammite woman distressed about her beloved. In a dream, she could not find him in the place where she dwelt. The lover was used to having him near her. Longing for his presence, she panicked and then suddenly arose crying, "I will get up now and go about the city, through its streets and squares" (Song of Sol. 3:2a). Then she actually found him on the streets. This serves as a prophetic picture for today: In this hour, we will find the Lord's manifest presence more on the streets, in the marketplace, and among the lost than in church buildings.

Please understand, I am not saying God is going to abandon His local church, and neither should we walk away from a commitment to our local church families. The Lord will always be with His people. Believers are called to congregate together as often as possible, especially in these last days. Jesus will be with His people wherever they are, but His manifest glory and active grace will now be more tangible when the Church is amidst the lost. Just as a farmer's house and barn get emptied of laborers who go to the fields, we will see churches emptying to head toward the lost. The harvest all comes back to the barn in the end, and then his house is once again full. Church leaders who will thrust members out into the fields white with harvest will see their churches overflowing. Others who attempt to hold on to old ways, programs, and church members will be very disappointed by the resulting dissipation of interest, anointing, and congregational membership.

LIGHT BELONGS IN THE DARKNESS

Isaiah 61:1 says, "The Spirit of the Lord God is upon me *because* the Lord has anointed me to bring good news to the poor." If we are going to see a great harvest, then we need to understand the power of the light we are carrying. Christ in us is that light! We have been anointed by the Spirit to bring good news to the afflicted (some Bible versions say "the poor"). If we bring the light of the gospel of Christ into the deepest, darkest places of society, then we will see revival and harvest. This is what the Church is made for!

Oftentimes, we find Christians and churches moving into middle-class suburbia and the most comfortable places in society. Of course, this is not wrong in itself, especially if we have been specifically called to these areas. However, if we attempt to hide ourselves in a sterile environment, we are missing something quite clear in Scripture. In Western countries, we seldom hear about powerful moves of the Spirit accompanied by miracles, signs, and wonders. We seldom hear testimonies of hundreds of thousands of souls coming to know Christ in a single gathering, as is the case in many impoverished nations. Why is that? Because we stay in our church services instead of going to where the afflicted need God's touch. If we want to see the anointing in full operation, we need to look for the afflicted, the broken, the destitute, and the poor. We need to leave our comfortable environments and go to the darkness.

INCARNATIONAL EVANGELISM

Danielle Strickland and her husband, Stephen Court, minister with the Salvation Army. They are full of gospel fire! A few years ago, they moved into the sin-infected, inner city of Vancouver with their newborn son, Zion. Their vision was to engage in *incarnational evangelism*, which meant to live among those in the drug-infested, corrupt, and violent downtown. This is similar to what Jesus did when He left His glorious dwelling in Heaven and came to sinful earth. He not only dwelt among us, but He actually became one of us, yet without sin. Incarnational evangelism is about identifying with the sinner to bring light into the darkness.

THE NEW WINESKIN

Steve and Danielle had a vision to build a new wineskin. They don't have a church building, but their team effectively builds relationships and Christian community in the inner city. They reside in slum hotels and co-ops, eat meals in mission houses, and live among addicts, prostitutes, murderers, and thieves. The Lord is moving among them powerfully as they see the region transformed one day and one life at a time. Someone approached Danielle and asked her, "Where is your church?" She responded, "You're looking at it." We *are* the Church. The Church is not what we do or where we go; it is who we are. Church as we know it today is going to look quite different tomorrow. How is it going to look? I don't exactly know—I just know that it is going to be different. As we walk with the Holy Spirit, that new reality will become more visible.

Jesus taught that a new wineskin is needed to hold new wine (see Matt. 9:17). In these coming hours, some of what the Lord will call us to do has never been done before. We cannot think according to old patterns or methods, we need to draw near to God for His inspiration and instruction. If we are going to run into the darkest of places with the torch of His love, then we must have His divine strategies. In a prophecy brought by Stacey Campbell a few years ago, the Lord said, *"Somebody's got to create a container for the time, and they can't go to the past to look for it. Some of it has never been done before and especially in this final hour."*

Flexibility and openness of heart to hear what the Lord is saying to the Church will be key in this season. We cannot hold on to old forms and structures if the Lord is not telling us to do so. But people often find change difficult. I remember hearing a story once about a pastor who accepted a senior position in a church. He noticed that the grand piano was on his left side of the podium. As he preached, he tended to favor his right side. So, the solution was simple: He moved the piano to the other side of his podium. The next Sunday, the congregation was in an uproar over the move. After all, the piano had always been on the other side. They actually made the pastor move the piano back because they couldn't cope with the change.

Being a man of wisdom and great patience, the pastor decided to make the change a little slower so as to cultivate flexibility in the congregation. Every week, he moved the piano a few inches. Within a year or so, he had moved the piano to the platform's other side and the congregation was fine with the change—in fact, they didn't even notice. Some changes might be coming to what we know now as church, so let's be willing to follow the Holy Spirit into the formation of a new wineskin.

CHURCH IN THE COFFEE SHOP

One night, I was out with a few friends doing some television filming on the streets of Toronto. Finishing close to midnight, we entered a 24-hour café in the inner city to warm up and drink some coffee. We decided to take our television camera with us, rather than leave it in the car where it could be vulnerable to theft. When we entered the coffee shop, you could feel tension in the air. The customers, who mainly consisted of addicts and homeless people, were not at all happy about the camera's presence. They all watched us with suspicion.

Finally one gentleman came to us and said, "What are you up to?" We responded, "We're having a cup of coffee." He then inquired, "What's with the camera?" We explained to him about *Extreme Prophetic* and our plans to minister to the city's homeless people with a large group of local Christians. As part of our preparation, we were scouting the area and getting some footage. As we continued to chat with the man, his guard slowly came down. Before we knew it, he was sharing some of the deepest secrets of his life. Others in the shop were watching and listening with curiosity. After about an hour, he allowed us to pray and prophesy over him and then he came into faith. When the man left, he was really happy.

Suddenly I heard, "Psst, psst, psst," from another table. The whispers came from a homeless man who had been listening to our conversation. As I approached him, he said, "Does the Good Lord have a word for me too?" I responded, "He sure does." I proceeded to prophesy over him and his girlfriend. Then others in the shop asked for prayer and prophetic ministry, even the employee working behind the counter. Before we knew it, a Holy Spirit initiated "church" gathering had erupted after midnight in a 24-hour, inner-city coffee shop, and we didn't even have to rent the building! We had shared the Word, glorified God, prayed, prophesied, and encouraged people to believe in Christ. Wow, now that's church! It might not look like it in the traditional sense, but it's church!

GET YOUR RUNNING SHOES ON

Everything that transpired that evening was led and directed by the Holy Spirit. All we did was follow His leading and unction. We simply carried the Christ who dwells within us into the darkness. As we follow the Holy Spirit, He will lead and guide us into the fullness of the harvest. He will enable us to hold the torch up high and run our race with a fresh fervency of heart. We will run with the vision. The light of Christ Himself *is* the vision. Through His Church, He will illuminate the entire world with His love and glory. You, I, and all His people are being called. Get your running shoes on and run with the vision. The race is beginning.

3

CHAPTER

The Highway Byway Revival

So those servants went out into the
highways and gathered together all
whom they found... (Matthew 22:10, nkj)

In the darkness of Vancouver's inner-city streets and alleys lurked devastated lives. Words fail to describe the depravity I witnessed while walking through the region in February 2004. Was this state of degeneracy even possible in North America? The city's inner core is a "free-zone" for drug use. Canada does have laws forbidding the sale and use of street drugs, but the law is overlooked in this particular location and the addicts are well aware of it. Law enforcement and judicial systems cannot keep up with all the criminal activities, so they attempt to localize the hard-core problems by excusing it in this region.

As a result, it is not uncommon to see people shooting up heroin, sniffing glue, and smoking marijuana or crack cocaine. All of this activity is going on right in the open as you walk down the street. On one occasion, some Christians witnessed to four young people who were smoking a three-foot crack pipe in public view, all while they bragged about their experience. A familiar sight is to see people passed out and overdosed on drugs in alleyways and sometimes on open sidewalks of the main roads. People walk over and drive by these breathing corpses as if the situation is normal.

An absence of law enforcement also leaves prostitutes to sell themselves on the corners of every street in the inner city. Months and years of abuse and addiction have left them as completely wasted individuals. Prostitutes are constantly picked up on street corners, most often by middle-class men. Oftentimes, just as many walk the streets in early morning and midday as during nighttime.

Homeless people looking for refuge from the cold are frequently found sleeping in shopping carts full of their personal items. Others who missed getting into the shelters find pieces of old carpet or collapsed cardboard boxes to protect them from the cold. Being asked for money is a normal occurrence when you walk down inner-city streets. Money is needed for food, drink, bus fares, and places to stay. Most of the time, of course, the financial blessing put into their hands goes straight toward their drug habits. Lying, stealing, and cheating is a way of life for people on these streets because it is how they survive.

Danger and violence prevail in the inner city and its atmosphere is permeated with a stench of death. A day doesn't go by without violent crime or a death by murder, suicide, or drug overdose. We stayed in a slum hotel for several days to identify with those who live in the region. Throughout the night, we heard gun shots and people screaming in terror. Loud alarms from burglar systems and screaming sirens of police cars, ambulances, and other emergency vehicles were familiar sounds, both day and night.

One of our team members once watched as a man splattered onto the pavement after jumping from a three-story window. Although still breathing, he had blood seeping out of his ears, nose, and mouth. As our team member prayed for him while awaiting an ambulance, some street addicts ran into his room and grabbed a television and other personal items that they could sell for their own personal drug needs. They ran right past the man's dying body while carrying these stolen goods. No value was placed on his life. None of his street buddies seemed to care if he lived or died. This is life in the darkness.

Children in the inner city are definitely at risk. They are never seen playing on the street. In fact, children are hardly ever seen at all, but they are there. Often, they get locked up to care for themselves in slum houses, apartments, or hotel rooms, while their mothers are out turning tricks or buying the next fix. Typically, their fathers are long gone. Children here are sexually, emotionally, and physically abused and neglected at a young age. Inner-city playgrounds are littered everywhere with hypodermic needles. After shooting up drugs, addicts carelessly leave them lying around. Although programs exist to help clean up the playground, the problem is far from rectified.

CAN DRY BONES LIVE?

I became undone while walking those streets. The consequence of sin surrounded me in measures that the average person never sees in an entire lifetime. I certainly wasn't used to experiencing such degradation. But all the deep, ugly darkness was hidden and tucked away in a world-renowned city otherwise full of beauty. All very vivid and so in my face was a dark pit of a place with real people trapped in real bondage because of real sin.

I deeply wanted to feel God's heart on this issue. I knew He hated the sin that trapped these people, yet He loved each one more than they could ever know. Society has written them off, legal systems have given them up, the middle class has shunned them, the rich despise them, and the corrupt use them. In many ways, the Church has ignored them, but God loves them. Dead yet breathing, they exist in a living hell. Oh God, what can we do?

I thought of the prophecy found in Ezekiel 37. God showed the prophet a vision of a valley full of dry, dead, and disjointed bones. God then asked Ezekiel, "Son of man, can these bones live?" If looking at these lifeless bones through natural vision, you would tend to say, "Are you kidding?" But Ezekiel was a prophet, and prophets are seers who peer beyond the outward appearance into God's will and potential. Ezekiel responded, "O Sovereign Lord, You alone know."

God's answer to Ezekiel was for him to prophesy words of life and destiny. God is a creator and a restorer of all and nothing is impossible for Him. Ezekiel began to prophesy and, suddenly, the unthinkable happened: With a rattling noise, the bones started coming together—it was the sign of revival. The bones came together, took shape, and became covered with sinew and skin. As Ezekiel continued to prophesy, breath came into the bones and they were raised into a great army, full of life, power, potential, and a future.

Part of our mandate as Christians is to raise the dead who are now walking the highways and byways. These living dead have no life and no hope, but God is able to raise them up. The "breathing dead" are not just in the inner city, but exist everywhere. Perhaps they are your neighbors, your coworkers, your banker, or your grocer. That evening, however, as I observed the wreckage that surrounded me on the inner-city streets, I was hit hard by the deep reality of death's stench.

While praying, a prophetic vision showed me "the spirit of revival" touching the deepest, darkest places of our nations. I saw dry bones come to life as the power of God transformed the vilest sinners into vessels of righteousness. I saw the Church loosed into the streets in a power of revival that set captives free and fulfilled the Great Commission. This is what we, as believers, are made for. No matter how rebellious they are, God cares deeply for each individual. He knows each one by name, and He knows all the issues of pain that led them down a destructive path. Through outward appearance, you cannot always identify obvious value in a street person. But God sees their enormous worth and potential and He also wants us to see that. The Lord wants to set them free and He wants to use us for their release.

POSSESS AND OCCUPY

As I continued to pray while on the streets, the words "possess and occupy" repeatedly came to mind. In the Old Testament, we read how God led Israel into the Promised Land. Although they were promised Canaan, the Israelites had to conquer each city one at a time. Joshua led them to possess the gates of their enemies and then to occupy the territory. In other words, the cities they conquered became theirs to fully occupy and rule.

At that moment, an idea came to my mind: What would it look like if, all of a sudden, 100 Spirit-filled Christians moved into this sinfully dark environment? Immediately, the Lord's presence in that area would increase. Then, each of these Christians should commit to building a relationship with one lost soul. If, within a month, they won them to Christ, and then discipled them, there would be 200 Christians shining as lights in the darkness. That is a 100 percent increase in the number of believers occupying the area. If, in the next month, those 200 Christians repeated the same plan, you would have 400 Christians who illuminated the region.

Using the same strategy on the following month would mean 800 and, subsequently, 1600, 3200, 6400, and then 12,800 Christians. The inner city would then be filled to overflowing with the Holy Spirit's presence like never before. For sure, the tangible power of God would increase if each Christian committed to daily prayer, uncompromised devotion, righteous living, and a radical, focused outreach in the power of His love, mercy, and miracle-working anointing.

Imagine what a holy street invasion would look like. What if, as a missionary mandate, Christians deliberately flooded into inner cities to secure employment in law enforcement, courts, social work structures, post offices, restaurants, stores, rehab centers, medical clinics, and schools? What if, through their presence and prayers, these *missionaries* influenced every person with whom they came into contact? What if each of these *missionaries* believed God for a display of miracle deliverance, healing, salvation, and resurrection? Visualize the dead literally being raised to life on the streets. Envision the sick being healed by the supernatural power of God. Dare to picture drug addicts miraculously set free without any withdrawal symptoms. We have witnessed some of this already, but consider if this were a daily occurrence through every believer living or laboring in the region. Imagine an inner city full of intercession and healing rooms, prophetic booths, free deliverance prayer and counseling offices.

With unity of vision and focus among a growing number of believers, the tangible, manifest power of God grows exponentially. But you don't have to set out with a large group. Begin with a couple of people with a clear vision and strategy for increase and multiplication. You don't need to operate in great faith and power at first, but start with what you have and contend for increased grace. Perhaps our vision and faith are too small for what God desires to accomplish in our day. What would your city be like if the spirit of revival conquered the darkest places? Imagine how the headlines of your local newspaper would read. Dream big and believe God! As I pondered the potential of such a revival, I thought, "This is easy," or at least, it seemed so in the visions of my mind. God is a great God. His power is awesome and His blood will save, heal, and deliver today. He can touch the Western world with revival power as easily as anywhere else. Bring it on, Lord!

I thought of Rolland and Heidi Baker who touch people's lives in Mozambique with daily doses of God's love. At the beginning of the revival, they simply gave out bread to the hungry in the garbage dump and brought orphaned street children into their own home. Each day, they reached out to the poor in spirit and God moved. Every day, they shared the gospel and led souls to Christ, and, every month, more workers relocated to Mozambique to join them.

Now, only a few years later, thousands of churches are planted to facilitate the hundreds of thousands of new converts. Local believers have been raised up by the thousands to engage in Kingdom ministry and advancement. Deliverance and healing miracles are a daily occurrence, and the dead are raised on a regular basis. Rolland, Heidi, and their team love them to life! What they are doing is Kingdom revival. The same God who is touching Mozambique and other places where the poor are crying out in the darkness will also touch us in the West.

Why the Inner City, the Poor, and the Afflicted?

Some of you may wonder why I am focusing on the inner city and depraved, poverty-stricken areas like Mozambique. You may want to see harvest in your middle-class suburb or among your wealthy friends and family. God is not a respecter of persons and, of course, He wants to reach everyone, including all those you hold a burden for. I am not suggesting that the inner city is the only place where God is going to move in power, but Scripture clearly indicates that the anointing is to be ministered to the afflicted and the poor.

The Spirit of the Lord is upon me, because He has anointed me to preach the good news to the poor. He has sent me to proclaim freedom for the prisoners and recovery

*of sight for the blind, to release the oppressed, to proclaim
the year of the Lord's favor* (Luke 4:18-19).

Many keys to revival and harvest lie in this passage of
Scripture. The word *because* is significant; the Spirit of the
Lord is upon us for a reason. Why? We are anointed. For what
purpose? To preach good news to the poor, proclaim release to
captives, give sight to the blind, set free the oppressed, and
proclaim the favor of the Lord.

Jesus also taught in Matthew 5:3, "Blessed are the poor in
spirit for theirs is the kingdom of heaven." Putting these Scriptures together reveals that the anointing will manifest strongest
when we go to the poor, the captives, the blind, and the
oppressed. Anyone who doesn't identify their poverty of spirit
will not see the Kingdom of Heaven manifest in their life.
Many rich and good-living people are poor in spirit. They have
yet to know the way of salvation and will probably not be
touched by truth until seeing depravity within their own soul.
We can still pray, however, that they will see the truth.

On the other hand, folks trapped in inner cities have no
problem seeing their degradation; they know themselves to be
poor, afflicted, and bound. Therefore, the anointing will flow in
greater measures in these areas, if we move into the fulfillment
of our calling.

In Matthew 22:2-10, Jesus shares a parable about the
Kingdom of Heaven. He said that it could be compared to a
king who gave a wedding feast for his son. He sent out invita-
tions to many guests, but they would not come. Instead, each
of them went about their own business. The enraged king sent
his slaves to the highways and byways to invite all they found,
both the good and the evil. As a result, the wedding hall was
filled with dinner guests. I believe this parable is a prophetic
picture of the revival that will take place on the streets in this
hour. It is time for us to go to the highways and byways and

compel the lost to come in. Now is time to go into the deepest, darkest places to share the light and life of Christ.

The inner city is much like our inner man. When Christ came into our life, the Spirit of Jesus possessed and occupied our spirit (or inner man). As a result, He influenced our entire being. Perhaps when the inner city is possessed and occupied by the Spirit of God, the entire region will also be touched by His glory and presence. Maybe this is a good reason to go to the darkest places of our communities and let our light shine. After all, light belongs in the darkness.

REACHING THE RICH THROUGH THE POOR

When revival and harvest break out in dark places amongst the poor and the afflicted, the rich also will be impacted. Mother Teresa is one of my heroes. She was a humble servant of the Lord who cared for the afflicted and the poor like no one else in our day. She identified with them and laid her life down to touch them with comfort, provision, and mercy. Most of her ministry was centered in India among the poorest of the poor. Yet, she was probably one of the most influential individuals in our lifetime amongst wealthy and prestigious people. She influenced economic, academic, political, and religious leaders. She spoke before presidents, kings, prime ministers of nations, and leaders of global political institutions. She caught the attention of both the rich and the famous. Why? Simply because she was doing what we are called to do when the Spirit of the Lord is upon us. As she ministered to the poor and the afflicted, God then, in turn, touched the rich. People who stood before Mother Teresa said they felt as if they were standing in the presence of Jesus Himself. The anointing and the glory was strong upon her. The Spirit of the Lord rested on her because she had an anointing to minister to the poor and the afflicted.

I highly respect Heidi and Rolland Baker as well as other ministers like Jackie Pullenger, author of *Chasing the Dragon* and long-time missionary to the opium addicts who lived in a dark, walled city in Hong Kong. They have given their lives to the poor, the oppressed, and the broken. As a result, they have amazing influence amongst the rich, and it is not because they intentionally focus on ministering to the rich. But middle-class and well-to-do people get touched by the testimony and anointing of God that flows through them to the afflicted. This is a Bible principle: Believers operating in supernatural Kingdom power accomplish what man never could in his own strength. Such is the grace that comes when we are willing to bring light into the darkness.

I gladly cheer on those ministering to the well-to-do and the satisfied of soul. I fully believe that every class of people needs to be reached. God calls us to various fields and we all need to be faithful to where He calls us. Many, however, who have much in the area of the world's goods are not yet ready for the Lord's touch on their lives. Those who find satisfaction in their good works and fulfilling lifestyles are not often prepared to surrender all to Him. But many poor and afflicted are ready to give it all to Jesus—now! Let's look for those who are acquainted with their personal depravity. These individuals can be found in any neighborhood and in every walk of life. Reaching them with the anointing is why the Spirit of the Lord is upon us.

WE MUST GO

Regardless of whether we are burdened for the destitute in the inner city, the elite of society, or all who are in between, we need to understand this: God loves the sinner, no matter what shape, size, or container they come in. He has set a banquet of His mercy and goodness for each one and He wants His house full. This is a "go season" and the Lord has said, "Go ye into all the world" (Mark 16:15, KJV). He didn't say, "Stay ye in all the church."

He is calling us to compel the lost to come into His Kingdom. He has called us to go into the highways and byways and invite all to the feast of His deep and amazing love. He doesn't want even one to be lost. This is a harvesttime for God to move in revival on the streets. Let's go into the darkness and spread His light. Let's begin a highway, byway revival.

A PROPHECY THROUGH STACEY CAMPBELL

Stacey Campbell proclaimed the following prophetic word regarding a "Highway, Byway Revival," which is a powerful message for the Church. May you be deeply inspired and touched by these words.

Jesus replied: "A certain man was preparing a banquet and invited many guests. At the time of the banquet he sent his servant to tell those who had been invited to, 'Come for everything is now ready.' But they all began to make excuses. The first said, 'I have just bought a field and I must go and see it, so please excuse me.' The second said, 'I have just bought five yoke of oxen, and I must go and try them out. Please excuse me.' Still another said, 'I just got married, so I cannot come.' The servant came back and reported this to his master. Then the owner of the house became angry and ordered his servant to go quickly into the streets and alleys of the town and to bring in the poor, the crippled, the blind, and the lame. 'Sir,' said the servant, 'what you have ordered has been done, but there is still room.' The master told the servant, 'Go out to the roads and country lanes, into the highways and the byways and make them, compel them to come in, so that my house will be full'" (Luke 14:16-23).

Then I heard what sounded like a great multitude, like the roar of rushing waters and the loud peals of thunder, shouting: Hallelujah! For the Lord God Almighty reigns. Let us rejoice and be glad and give Him glory, for the wedding of the Lamb has come and the bride has made herself ready. It was given to her to clothe herself in fine linen, bright and clean, and the fine linen stands for the righteous acts of the saints (Revelation 19: 6-8).

As we near the end of the age, I believe that the understanding of love—of bridal love— will be so deepened that the Bride will long to make herself look like the Bridegroom. She will begin to prepare herself in a wedding gown that is so pure, that is so filled with righteous acts, that is so white and holy, that her very garment will begin to reflect the great love of the Bridegroom.

And, at that time, the Bridegroom will give a revelation to the Bride like she has never had before of how great is His Love and how big is His Heart. So, that the Bride will begin to catch it and capture it and begin to look just like the Bridegroom. Out of that love, she will go into places where she has never gone before. She will go out to the poor, and to the blind, and to the crippled, and to the lame, and she will begin to go out and she will begin to increase in righteous acts.

And then the Bridegroom will gaze at His Bride and the Bride will gaze at the Bridegroom, and the love between them will be so intense that the greater love that Jesus spoke of will begin to flourish in the Bride, and she will begin to lay her life down in unprecedented fashion for those who cannot pay her back.

She will begin to look just like Jesus did on the Cross. And the understanding of love that looks like a Cross will hit the Church for those who have ears to hear. And the greater love and the greater works will begin to flourish and to flow in the Church. And greater love has no man than this than He lays

His life down for His friends, and we are His friends, if we do what He asks (see John 15:13-14).

There will be a harvest at the end of the age that will come through those servants who are willing to go where Jesus has called them to go—to places where the Cross will be the most evident, to the highways and to the byways and to the places where no one else will go, to the crosses of the earth.

So, the Lord is issuing us a challenge. He is saying, "Come, for all things are now ready and the time of My great banquet is approaching. Prepare yourselves in that wedding gown; make yourself ready and fill yourselves with righteous acts that will reflect My Glory—the glory of compassion, mercy, loving-kindness, truth, forgiveness, and justice. Prepare yourselves, for I too am preparing for that day."

4

CHAPTER

Prophetic Evangelism

...THE TESTIMONY OF JESUS IS THE SPIRIT OF PROPHECY (REVELATION 19:10).

One of the greatest power tools for evangelism is the gift of prophecy. Its wide use on the streets is bringing in a great harvest. Ministers, such as John Paul Jackson, are launching out teams that use dream interpretations to touch the masses. They go into major national and international events and reach the unsaved. Doug Addison is a minister who utilizes the prophetic gift to reach the New Age and occult community. Graham Cooke prophesies over businessmen and even teaches unsaved entrepreneurs how to hear God for themselves; as a result of his efforts, many are getting saved. Bill Johnson's Bethel Church in Redding, California, is a forerunner in prophetic evangelism, both on the streets and amongst business people. Still others minister prophetically to political leaders and high-profile people in the movie industry. Media prophets are also being raised up to prophesy to the lost. The concept of using the prophetic gift in evangelism is spreading rapidly and is proving very effective. Prophecy is a *now gift* for the harvest season.

From the moment I was born again, I had a passion to reach the lost. Even as a young Christian, I led evangelism teams into the streets. In those days, the custom was to grab handfuls of gospel tracts and use them to share the good news with those who were interested. Our style was aggressive and focused. We believed in the prophetic and the miraculous, and definitely ministered these graces whenever the doors opened. Mostly, however, we demonstrated the gifts in our circles among believers. As passionate as I was for bringing souls to Christ, the thought never crossed my mind of actually asking people on the street if they would like a prophetic word of encouragement.

For the first 14 years of my life with Christ, I ate, slept, and breathed evangelism. I loved reaching the lost and bringing souls into the Kingdom. In 1990, however, everything changed almost overnight. After a 12-month season of service in Mexico, Ron and I returned to our home in Canada. My practice had been to engage in daily evangelism outreach of some sort—but now something had changed. I seemed to have lost motivation, and I no longer had any anointing or favor on the streets. No one was interested in listening to me and no one was receiving Christ.

When I ministered inside the church, however, I was blessed with fruit and tangible anointing. But on returning to the streets, I found myself to be dry and empty. I was puzzled and began to wonder if I had backslidden. One day, the Lord spoke to me and said, "I am taking you out of evangelism (laboring with the lost) for a season and am calling you to serve in revivalism (serving the Body of Christ)."

I assumed this "season" would be for three months, just as in the natural seasons, but God's timing is very different from ours. For 12 years, I ended up serving in the church and I engaged in very little ministry to the lost during that time. In winter 2000, I was awakened to an understanding of a new wineskin for evangelism. Walter Heidenreich, an apostle and dear friend from Germany, was visiting our church in Kelowna, British Columbia. Due to a visitation of the Holy Spirit in 1987, our local church had become internationally renowned for its prophetic fluency. Walter applauded that any believer could come into our services or prayer meetings to receive encouraging prophetic words. "But," he added, "what about the lost? What about the unsaved? Why aren't Christians out in the malls and shops and everywhere else giving prophetic words?" Why wasn't our church? *Why wasn't I,* I wondered.

His message that evening convicted me deeply. As Christians, we are extremely blessed with prophetic encouragement when we need it. Even if the prophetic gift is not flowing in our local churches, we can easily access encouragement through ministries like Steve Shultz's Elijah List. What is the answer for those who cannot hear God's voice for themselves because they do not know Him? What about those who have never had a prophetic blessing proclaimed over their lives? Walter's exhortation challenged me to step outside the safety of the believers' environment and use the prophetic gift to take Christ's love and encouragement into the streets.

I was willing to use the prophetic gift to reach the unsaved, so I prayed on the matter and invited the Lord to give me a strategy and some increased understanding. That prayer birthed our Extreme Prophetic schools. The whole idea behind Extreme Prophetic is to take God's prophetic gift with extreme love into extreme places, like the shops, the streets, or anywhere there are unsaved people. Our first school and outreach was held summer 2000. I asked Stacey Campbell and Todd Bentley to be involved, and both spoke and taught at the school where we trained 200 students in the prophetic. After asking God for creativity in reaching the lost, He gave us all sorts of extreme ideas.

FREE SPIRITUAL READINGS AT BOOSTER JUICE

Following classroom training, the school hosted about 12 different options for outreach. Stacey led a team that offered free spiritual readings at Booster Juice, a café in downtown Kelowna. We called them "spiritual readings" because the Holy Spirit warned us that the unsaved had issues with the church and religion. So, instead of making the outreach sound churchy or preachy, He told us that people would be more open to the prophetic if we just said something about the Spirit.

So, we decided on "Free Spiritual Readings." *Free*—because the gospel is free. Jesus said, "Freely you have received, freely give" (Matt. 10:8). *Spiritual*—because the Bible names gifts of the Spirit as *spiritual* gifts. *Readings*—because God reads destiny over our lives to proclaim hope and a future. We went all around town handing out and posting flyers that said, "Free Spiritual Readings at Booster Juice Today!" No one ever asked what a spiritual reading was, they just seemed to know and they definitely wanted one.

When we opened the café for prophetic ministry, people were lined up outside of Booster Juice for up to an hour-long wait. Stacey was leading two teams in the café. So many people wanted to receive a word that we had to add a third team. Eventually, we added two more prophetic ministry teams stationed in the corner of the shop. Even with a total of five teams, there was still a line-up of people—that's how many people, even in our little city of Kelowna, wanted to hear about God's plan for them.

One man on his lunch break waited about 45 minutes. He was very concerned about not getting his reading before having to go back to work, so he started asking people if he could move up in line. That's the type of hunger these people have.

One fellow who came in for a prophetic word appeared to be a really tough biker character. His huge arms were folded across his barrel of a chest. His face was stern, and his eyes were filled with hardness, desperation, and fear. Through a specific word of knowledge, he opened his heart to the Lord and received Jesus as his Savior. In that one outreach station alone, over seven people came to know the Lord. Many more were deeply touched by His love, all from a few hours at a juice café.

CREATIVE PROPHETIC OUTREACH

Other outreaches included a team that did prophetic sidewalk art drawings in chalk for young people at a skateboard park. Several prophetic art teams went out and prophesied destiny words over people with songs, poems, and portraits. One team even went to a public park and drew washable prophetic tattoos on children's arms, all while explaining the words of destiny that God was proclaiming over their lives. Their parents were very touched and the children delighted in their fresh "tatts."

A door-to-door team went through a neighborhood and prayed over each household. The next day, they went back with gifts for each home and shared the prophetic words and blessings they received from God. The people loved it. Most everyone opened up their doors to the teams and invited them to pray a blessing on their households.

IMPACTED BY THE PROPHETIC!

We were greatly encouraged on the evening prior to that first school outreach. A few of us from the school shared dinner at the home of Ralph and Donna Bromley, personal friends and leaders of an international organization that cares for orphans. For a number of months, the couple had hosted a Chinese foreign exchange student in their home. He was a self-proclaimed communist and, although extremely polite and gracious, he had chosen not to believe the gospel whenever they took an opportunity to share with him. That evening, the Chinese student was also a dinner guest.

While sharing light conversation around the meal, we made mention of the Free Spiritual Readings to be held at Booster Juice on the following day. Perplexed, the Chinese man interjected in somewhat broken English, "Ah, what are free spiritual readings?" We proceeded to share with him how God knows everything about everybody and He loves to encourage people with special words. We then simply asked him, "Can we practice on you?"

He responded with a measure of enthusiasm. Before we knew it, he was seated on a chair in the living room and we began to prophesy, and did so for more than forty minutes! The Lord revealed some very specific things about his past, future, personal dreams, as well as a number of intimate issues that no one except the Lord Himself could have known. By the end of the word, the astounded student shared his utter amazement. He then asked with deep sincerity, "What must I do now?"

That evening, Linda Palone, an enthusiastic evangelist, led the Chinese student to Christ. Days later, we prayed for him to receive the fullness of the Spirit with the evidence of speaking in tongues. A few weeks after, he invited some college friends to also enjoy some prophetic ministry. He said to them, "Ah, come to Bromley's for free spiritual reading." Four of them received prophetic ministry and were touched by the Lord in deep ways. In time, they also came to the Lord. The seed was planted that first night of dinner at the Bromley's house.

That was our launch and, since then, schools and accompanying outreaches have been taught every year. We have taken God's love and encouragement to the casinos and psychic shops of Las Vegas, the streets of Hollywood, the brothels of Amsterdam, the bathrooms of Kuwait, the drug-infested alleys of Vancouver, and all sorts of other extreme places. We have prophesied over the rich, the poor, the young, the old, the well-educated, and even the preschoolers. Many of our students caught the vision and took the idea to start up teams for prophetic outreach in their hometowns.

PSYCHIC FAIRS AND COMMUNITY EVENTS

Following the school, one woman set up Free Spiritual Reading booths in psychic fairs and community events. Long lines of people would stand waiting for their destiny words. Oftentimes, hundreds would come to Christ in a single four-day event.

Prophetic music artists are also taking their gift into the New Age environment. Norm Strauss, a prophetic musician, songwriter, and worship leader in our church in Kelowna, was actually invited to lead worship in a New Age church. They loved Norm and his music so much that they actually asked him back. Norm and his band also held home concerts for the unsaved. As they played prophetically and shared testimony, the Lord's power visited those meetings in very special ways.

A few of our team members went to a popular bookstore in our community and engaged in prophetic poetry readings during the monthly session when poets met. The unsaved were captured by the passion of our poems. As a result of words that touched their hearts in deep, intimate places, they were sometimes found weeping.

The vision for prophetic evangelism is spreading, and the lost love it! The unsaved are looking for a power greater than themselves. They are looking for words that will guide them into their destinies. The Church needs to be there to give them those words. If we don't, all they will know is the enemy's counterfeit: psychics, tarot card readers, palm readers, and other false prophetic expressions, which are everywhere. The difference between the true and the false is the Source. How will the masses discern the difference if they never experience the true? People are hungry for the prophetic and we, the Church, carry the true version within our spirits.

THE EXAMPLE OF JESUS

Perhaps the best example of prophetic evangelism in Scripture is found in John 4:1-42 when the Lord encounters the Samaritan woman at the well. Jesus had been on a journey and was weary from His travels, so He stopped by a well for refreshment. Note that He was not in a synagogue, temple, or a church; He was out on the streets in a public place. When the woman came to the well to draw water, Jesus initiated a conversation that resulted in His disclosing some prophetic revelation. She was amazed that He could know such intimate details about her life. The prophetic insight warmed the woman and made her open her heart. Then He revealed Himself as the Messiah. Immediately, the woman became an evangelist. She believed Jesus and, as a result, left her waterpot and went to preach to the men of the city. They responded to her zealous invitation and journeyed to see Him. Verse 39 says, "Many of the Samaritans from that town believed in Him because of the woman's testimony...." She became a prophetic evangelist. Indeed, the testimony of Jesus is the spirit of prophecy! (See Revelation 19:10.)

The best part of the Samaritan woman's outreach follows in verses 41 and 42: "And because of His words many more became believers. They said to the woman, 'We no longer believe just because of what you said; now we have heard for ourselves, and we know that this man really is the Savior of the world.' "The prophetic opened the door to their hearts and carried the seed of revelation that Jesus Christ was their Deliverer and Messiah. Upon this revelation, they believed unto salvation.

The most wicked of sinners is only one revelation away from salvation. All an individual needs to receive Christ is for the light of revelation to be turned on inside the heart. This is what brings conviction. Once they receive that illumination, faith will be birthed. It is all that you and I needed to be saved. The conviction for any level of rebellion and lawlessness is found in the revelation of Christ, who is Himself the Truth. The prophetic gift is a powerful tool for opening hearts.

IN THE PARK

While Donna Bromley and I were overseeing teams during a school outreach, we ventured out to see if any of the various groups needed help. We arrived at a park that was one of the stations for the outreach. On the grass sat a group of young ruffians. I said to Donna, "Would you like to have some fun?" So, we proceeded toward where they were seated. "Hey, guys," I said with childlike excitement in my 50-plus-year-old body. "We are from a school in town and are learning how to hear special words of destiny from God. He knows everything about your past, present, and future. Would you mind if we practiced on you?"

They mocked and scorned us, but I proceeded to press in. "Even if just one of you would let us try, it would be helpful."

One of the young men had his arms folded and, with a bit of hesitation, said, "You can give me a try. Are you psychic or something?"

With obvious excitement, I thanked him for the opportunity. Then, I explained that we weren't psychic, but that God Himself, who knew everything, would reveal the words to us. I told him that I needed to pray, ask God for the word, and wait for His answer.

"Whatever!" he replied with a little impatience.

I bowed my head and prayed and silently cried out to the Lord in desperation, "Oh God, You better give me something because right now I feel absolutely empty!" Within seconds, I received a mental impression from the Lord. "Wow, I'm getting something! It's really happening," I said excitedly.

"What are you getting?" the young man inquired.

I replied, "Well, I see a vision of a basement suite. I think you live in a basement suite, and a little while ago you had something stolen from you." (The Lord had revealed that a bag of marijuana had been stolen, but I chose not to reveal those details to him.) "And then, I see that you found out it was your friend who stole it and that hurt you a lot because you had really tried to help this friend."

"You're freaking me out!" he shouted.

I responded, "Why? Did I say something wrong?"

He replied, "No, that really happened! What else is He tellin' ya."

Continuing to minister words, I said, "Well, He's showing me that He understands exactly how you feel because He gets taken advantage of all the time too. People mistreat Him constantly and all He ever does is treat everyone well. He understands how hurt you are!"

While his friends listened intently, we continued to minister more prophetic encouragement. At the end, I asked him, "Well, how did we do? On a scale of one to ten, what do you think?"

He replied, "Oh, it's a ten!" His enthusiastic response meant that we didn't need to recruit any more "volunteers." Another young man said with eagerness, "You can do me next."

One by one, we prophesied over all of them, except for one. During the entire time, one young man had been very belligerent and obnoxious. Although he was mocking and resisting, I actually wanted to prophesy over him more than all the others.

After we had finished ministering to everyone else, the Lord spoke strongly to my heart, "Do *not* prophesy over him." The message was strong and clear. We don't need signs and wonders from Heaven or strong confirmations to preach the gospel. We are already commissioned through words spoken by Jesus some 2,000 years ago. Neither do we need a specific word to release us to prophesy because the Scriptures exhort us to do so. During our time on earth, we are to steward the gospel well, invest the gifts, and be careful not to bury them. This is what pleases the Lord, but when the Lord says, "No," there is always a good reason.

All the young men were glowing following their prophetic words and they aggressively encouraged the *resister* to partake. In the midst of this, I looked at my watch and said, "Oops, we've got to get going. We are late for our reporting session."

One of them asked, "What about Kevin over here? He didn't get a word yet."

He continued to aggressively mock us, but inside I knew Kevin actually did want a prophetic word. However, I stood firm on the Lord's word, and merely replied, "We're sorry, we really need to get going." They all stood there waving good-bye. The spiritual atmosphere around them had changed. We didn't lead any of them to Christ that day, but we planted many seeds that opened their hearts to Truth.

We returned to the classroom and shared our testimony along with others who had been out prophesying. The next day, a group of some students from Holland were on their way to go cliff jumping. In order to get to the cliffs, they had to walk through a park. On their way, they saw a group of young guys sitting on the grass and decided to do some spiritual readings. The Dutch students approached the fellows, explained that they were being trained on how to hear God's voice, and asked if they could "practice" on them.

Surprised, the young guys said, "Some blond-haired ladies were in another park yesterday where we were and they did that God-word stuff. Are you from the same school?" The team from Holland immediately figured out that this was the same gang of "ruffians" we had shared with on the day before.

Kevin, the mocking young man who God told me not to give a word, said excitedly, "They didn't 'do' me yesterday." The students prophesied over Kevin and some others, brought three souls to faith in Christ, and invited them to come to church the next day.

PROPHETIC TRANSFERENCE ON THE STREETS

Following a conference gathering in Nashville with James Goll, a few of us decided to take a couple of young people out on the streets. Although it was late at night, the streets were buzzing with activity. Anticipating some God-appointments, we took our television camera with us. The first person whom we prophesied over was a Christian playing his guitar on a street corner. As we prophesied over the guitarist and filmed the encounter with the camera, some people began to rally around to ask us what we were doing. Before long, we were all engaged in prophesying on the streets. At one point, a small line-up of folks was waiting for a prophetic word.

One fellow had been encouraged by a friend to get a prophecy. He didn't know if he truly believed in what was going on, but his friend's persistence made him willing to wait. So we prayed over him and delivered some prophetic encouragement. The skeptical man was not at all impressed. He stated, "Ah, anyone could give me a word like that. How do I know it's God? It's too general. Tell me something more specific." Again, we prayed and gave another word that didn't seem to satisfy him.

Although he gave us a fairly rough response, we just responded with humility and gentleness. I said, "Well, we've done our best to hear a blessing word for your life. We are sorry if it doesn't touch you in a special way. God loves you very much."

I was ready to move on, when the next guy in line (an obvious sinner who had been smoking marijuana) stepped up to the plate. He said, "You know, I have an opinion about this I'd like to share. I think God's trying to speak to you and He's trying to use these people to help. But you're not listening! Maybe you've got some kind of hurt or something and you've built a wall around your heart. That's what I think. I think you should listen to these good people!" He then stepped back in the line to take a drag off his "cigarette."

Even King Saul became prophetic when he hung out with the prophets. Peter prophesied that the Spirit would be poured out upon all mankind. Even the lost can prophesy when in an atmosphere of the prophetic.

A GREAT KEY

The prophetic is a great key for opening hearts to the truth of the gospel. One prophetic word can change a person's life forever. How you express the prophetic isn't what really matters. You can share prophetic encouragement through drawing, written poems or notes of blessing, approaching people on the streets, going door-to-door, singing prophetic songs, or any other creative means directed by the Holy Spirit. What matters is that you lean into God and simply step up and step out. Open your ears to hear His voice and share His love and encouragement wherever you are. In the next chapter, you will see just how simple it can be to prophesy.

5

CHAPTER

Prophesying Is Easy!

FOR YOU CAN ALL PROPHESY...
(1 CORINTHIANS 14:31).

So often, the prophetic carries a mystical and frightening edge in people's minds. Actually, all Christians have the ability to prophesy. It is very simple and natural when you understand what the Scriptures reveal concerning the prophetic. First Corinthians 14:31 states, "For you can all prophesy in turn so that everyone may be instructed and encouraged." The apostle Paul also exhorted believers to "eagerly desire spiritual gifts, especially the gift of prophecy" (1 Cor. 14:1). In Webster's Dictionary, the word *prophecy* is defined as "the gift of speaking under the influence of the Holy Spirit." In Acts 2:17, Peter prophesied that the Holy Spirit would be poured out upon all mankind in the last days, and, as a result, a whole lot of prophesying would be going on.

The Holy Spirit comes inside a person when they are born again. You cannot be born again without Him. Jesus told Nicodemus, "Flesh gives birth to flesh, but the Spirit gives birth to spirit" (John 3:6). In other words, your spirit man gets born again when the Holy Spirit enters. The Holy Spirit is the

Spirit of Jesus Christ. (The baptism of the Holy Spirit is yet another subject as it pertains to an infilling of the Holy Spirit's empowerment in spirit, soul, and body.)

Inherent to the Holy Spirit are the gifts of the Holy Spirit. When you have Him, His gifts are dwelling within you. A born-again believer then exercises these gifts by faith. The true gift of prophecy represents the heart and person of Jesus Christ as the inspiration is sourced within Christ's Spirit. The difference between true and false prophecy is its source. Psychic and occult prophetic practices have a source in either the human mind (psyche) or demonic spirits. Jesus Christ, however, is the source of true prophetic inspiration.

Prior to coming to Christ, I was involved in New Age and the occult. Although very fascinated by the various practices, I wasn't especially "spiritually sensitive," unlike many who had been aware of spiritual encounters from childhood. I was, however, very spiritually hungry. I signed up for various classes and learned how to move in New Age prophetic techniques. By applying various principles and engaging in activations, I became prophetic in expression. Such pursuits are dangerous because you yield to demonic spirits without realizing it. Most people in the New Age and occult community are very kind people and don't desire to hurt anyone. In fact, most of them are very loving, spiritually hungry people who do not realize they have stepped into deception.

Following my conversion, I renounced all occult and New Age practices due to the conviction of the Scriptures (see Deut. 18:9-14; Acts 19). I received deliverance ministry and was baptized with the Holy Spirit. A number of months following my deliverance, our church received teaching on the gifts of the Holy Spirit and *I learned* to prophesy. That's right, I learned. You too can learn and, as you read on, you will receive some keys in stepping out in faith to trust the Lord for prophetic expressions.

Many believe the gift of prophecy can only be exercised if an individual is empowered by the Holy Spirit at a special moment to prophesy. Although such an encounter would be completely valid, we must never limit God to only a sovereign visitation. He has invited us to access every covenant promise by faith. Through Christ's finished work on the Cross, every blessing has already been given to every believer (see Eph. 1:3; 2 Pet. 1:2-4).

A difference does exist between prophetic ability and the office of the prophet. The office gift is an actual appointment by God (not man) into position. Although God ordains the prophet into position, the prophet is still subject to the Body. There is no room for an independent spirit within the Kingdom of God. The prophet's role is not only to prophesy, but also to equip the Body of Christ so that all believers may grow in prophetic ability. The prophet in an office position has the ability to prophesy with authority, equip, and impart (see Eph. 4:11-13).

Prophetic expression, on the other hand, is something all believers can walk in. Prophecy is a gift from the Holy Spirit that is operated by faith. This gift operates through a believer's ability to not only hear or see the purposes of God, but also to communicate what is perceived. Jesus said, "My sheep listen to My voice; I know them, and they follow Me" (John 10:27). He also said, "But they will never follow a stranger; in fact, they will run away from him because they do not recognize a stranger's voice" (John 10:5). Again, I want to emphasize that the source of the true prophetic is the Holy Spirit and the testimony of Jesus (see Rev. 19:10). The false can be the carnal mind, the voice of the world, or the demonic. We need to learn to discern the true voice of God.

PROPHESYING IS EASY

Too often, we complicate our life in the Kingdom, when, in fact, the Lord has made everything simple for us to understand.

A Christ-directed life is easy to walk in, if we walk by faith according to His truth. The key to prophesying is simply to identify God's voice. We know that He speaks to His children, so it is just a matter of getting tuned in to His wavelength. Once you hear His voice, then you can communicate as He directs.

Some wonderful training classes are available to help believers step into the prophetic. Our ministry hosts a two-day boot camp that teaches basics of the prophetic, and it is amazing to see how quickly our students jump into the river of prophetic anointing. These boot camps are fun and informative. After taking these classes, most people realize that they have heard from God for years, but just hadn't recognized His voice.

PREPARING YOUR HEART TO PROPHESY

Development of godly character is the most important aspect about operating in the prophetic gift. The heart's motive must be pure, or the prophetic flow can be defiled. I liken this to a reservoir of water that is very pure at its source. For the reservoir water to supply you with a cup of drinking water, it must travel through pipes that lead to your faucet. With contaminated pipes, even water from a pure source gets defiled by the time it reaches your stomach. As a result, your body can be afflicted with symptoms of illness. So, the prophetic unction of the Holy Spirit can be pure at its source (in your spirit man), and yet be defiled if sin is in your life (rust in your pipes). The condition of our heart before God is always important. When ministering the prophetic gift to the unsaved, our character must exemplify the nature of Christ or our testimony will be tainted. If our hearts are not pure, instead of ministering life, we might minister defilement, judgment, or other ungodly characteristics.

1. A Single Heart

In preparing our heart to prophesy, we need to consider our commitment to the Lord. Does He have our full attention in life? Do we have other things or people that we love more than Him? To be effective in the prophetic, we must have a single focus. Jesus desires to have first place and longs to rule over our hearts with love and wisdom. We can take time each day in our devotions to reaffirm His position in our lives.

2. Posture

A posture of waiting on the Lord will allow us to hear His voice and receive from Him. Always being busy and having our minds engaged in affairs of everyday life makes it difficult to hear the Lord's voice. Too many distractions are a distraction. By posturing ourselves in submission to His Spirit, we can cultivate a precious relationship with the Lord.

3. Repentance From Sin

Take time to invite the Holy Spirit to convict you of any unconfessed sin. If you are made aware of something, then turn from that sin and ask for the Lord's forgiveness. First John 1:9 promises that "If we confess our sins, He is faithful and just and will forgive us our sins and purify us from all unrighteousness." Repentance removes any contamination that can block the prophetic from flowing.

4. Childlikeness

David said that "like a weaned child is my soul within me" (Ps. 131:2), and that he didn't concern himself with complicated matters. The prophetic word is best received when we embrace childlike simplicity. We are beloved covenant children who are heirs of His precious promises. Children don't strive—they trust and enjoy the benefits of their parent's provision.

5. Faith

Believe that you can prophesy. Remember that Ephesians 1:3 says that you are blessed with every spiritual blessing (including prophecy). Second Peter 1:3 informs us that we have been granted everything that pertains to life and godliness. You have everything you need to prophesy, but the gift must be activated by faith. When prophesying, believe that God speaks and that He will speak to you. Also, believe that He desires to bless the person you are ministering to; you can reach into God's heart and hear the special word for that person. Finally, believe that the Lord will enable you to deliver what He has revealed. The gift of prophecy is always operated by faith.

6. Humility and Servanthood

The prophetic gift is not to be used to puff up a minister's reputation. This gift allows you to serve others with the blessing of God. Prophesying to the unsaved is a tremendous privilege. Most non-believers have never known the honor of receiving a word of encouragement and love from the Lord. We are not to prophesy with an attitude or motive of flaunting prophetic ability. But, instead, we are to love and serve in a spirit of humility. We always point people to Jesus when prophesying.

7. Faithful in Little

When beginning to prophesy, you might feel as if you don't have very much to offer. When I began prophesying, I basically had one word that came to me most times. The word was very simple, yet extremely profound: "God loves you with an everlasting love." I didn't even realize that I prophesied this phrase over almost everyone.

After about a year of prophesying, a fellow in our church said to me, "You know, Patricia, I can almost prophesy what you are going to prophesy." That statement puzzled me, and then he proceeded to finish his thought by saying, "You are going to say something like, 'God really loves you.' You might even add, 'With an everlasting love!' " He chuckled and informed me that all my prophetic words sounded similar. I had no idea. Every time I ministered, the word felt fresh to me. With enthusiastic expectancy, I would wait on God; then I simply spoke what I felt Him say. My prophetic level was very simple, but, each time, I faithfully stepped out and believed God for a fresh word. After a while, I began to grow in prophetic fluency and authority. Having been faithful in little, God gave me increase.

In our prophetic evangelism training, we encourage fearful people to pull that old standby out of their heart if they get frozen when stepping out to prophesy to the lost. That special word—"God loves you with an everlasting love"—is true for all people and for all time. More than any other prophetic expression, I have seen those seven words consistently bring tears to people on the streets. The testimony of its power is amazing!

WAYS TO HEAR FROM GOD

God speaks to His people in many ways, but most predominantly through "God thoughts," which are pictures or impressions seen in the imagination. It might thrill you to know that many well-known prophets who carry tremendous authority in gift and office also receive most revelation through these two means. From time to time, they might also experience trances, open visions, angelic visitations, and audible voices. But the most common form of God communication is through thoughts and pictures.

1. God Thoughts

Your mind is an organ of the soul that God gave you for the purpose of enhancing relationship with Him. He has given you the ability to think and reason through your thoughts, which is the place where you will most often share communication with Him. The mind is a vital organ for spiritual growth. God speaks His thoughts into your mind consistently, so it is just a matter of learning to recognize them. Thoughts can come from your soulish nature, a demonic source, the world's influence, or the inspiration of the Lord, so we must to be able to recognize the source. A word from God is loving, righteous, kind, pure, aligned with truth, and full of wisdom and encouragement.

Our minds were never created to hold thoughts that didn't have God as their source. Due to the fall of mankind, however, sin entered in. Now, our thoughts often get polluted with what is not of the Spirit. In preparing to hear from God in your thoughts, take time to cleanse your mind and set it apart for the Lord's use. Invite Him to give you "God thoughts," and He will.

One way to strengthen your ability to receive God thoughts is to sit down with a journal and Bible and then ask the Lord questions, believing for an answer. This process is called "inquiring of the Lord." David often inquired of the Lord and so can you. Before you begin to inquire, pray for cleansing over your thoughts. Then, invite God to forgive you for any defiling thoughts that entered your mind up to that point. Declare to the enemy that "the voice of a stranger you will not hear." Bind satan's influence in

Jesus' name and cast down all thoughts that come from your carnal nature. Asking the Holy Spirit to fill your mind with His thoughts is what prepares you to hear from God.

You can ask Him simple questions like, "Do You love me?" Then, wait for the answer and write it down next to your question. Of course, that is a very general question and many already have such revelation, but it is a good place to start. You can proceed on to other questions that require a more specific answer. With a journal, you can keep track of the accuracy of your words. Always check your revelations to make sure they are not in violation of Scripture and the nature of God. The more you submit your spiritual hearing to the Lord, the more you will hear.

At a particular time in my walk with God, I desired to grow in more specific revelation. While sitting in a restaurant with some friends, I asked the Lord to reveal to me the waitress's favorite color. The thought came to mind, "red." I wrote the word down on my napkin and then asked Him to tell me her favorite meat. The thought "beef" came to me. She soon came by the table to take our orders. I asked her, "Excuse me, ma'am, but would you mind telling me what your favorite color is."

She said, "Sure, that would be red."

I was ecstatic! "Wow, I got it right!" I informed her with excitement. "I asked God to tell me what your favorite color was and He said, 'Red.' Look, I wrote it right here on my napkin. We're just learning how to hear the voice of God in a class we're taking [at that time, we were doing a School of Extreme Prophetic in Las Vegas] and I'm so glad I got it right."

She replied, "Really? That's cool. You mean, GOD actually told you my favorite color?"

Then I quizzed her, "Okay, what is your favorite meat?"

She answered, "Ah, let's see. That would be—chicken."

Looking at my previous prophetic answer, I explained, "Oh, I got that one wrong. I thought the Lord said *beef.*"

But then she responded, "Hey, wait a minute. It *is* beef. Filet mignon is my favorite meat. I forgot and said 'chicken' instead." The waitress then added, "Is He telling you anything else?" She came back to our table several times and received lots of good gospel input! Receiving revelation for the waitress was fun and, as a result, she became opened up to the Author of that revelation and allowed us to pray for her to receive Christ.

2. God Pictures

Just as the Lord places thoughts in our minds, He puts images in our imagination. Our imagination is a vision center created to receive pictures from God. You will never receive a visionary experience without the imagination being involved to some degree. The imagination is the place in your heart where you see vision.

Again, consecrating this organ is very important. In our life, we can be tempted to receive vain, evil, or lustful imaginations. Therefore, it is vital to receive cleansing by asking the Lord to forgive wrong imaginations and then to set ourselves apart, afresh for His purposes. As with the preparation process for the mind, make sure to take captive any demonic or carnal influence and bind the enemy from interjecting his images. One way to stir up your vision center is to meditate on prophetic visions in the Bible. Submit your imagination to visions of the prophets in the Word of God and attempt to see them in your mind's eye. Doing so will make your imagination more sensitive.

Ask the Lord to give you special pictures for people. One evening on Hollywood Boulevard, we had a nice conversation with a gentleman who did not know Christ. During our visit, God gave me a mental impression of a banquet table full of good food. Jesus then sat the man down at the table and began to serve him. As I communicated this *vision*, the man laughed. I then shared the interpretation with him. He asked me, "Do you want to know why I was laughing?"

I responded, "I sure do."

He then eagerly explained, "I serve banquets for a living." That little impression opened the man's heart to know how personal Jesus is, and he accepted Christ as Savior.

HOW DO YOU DISCERN THE TRUE FROM THE FALSE?

Often, people ask, "How can I know if what I'm receiving is of God?" That is a good question, and we always want to examine our source. The following are a few helpful plumblines to test true prophetic words.

It is unto edification, exhortation, and comfort. According to First Corinthians 14:3, your words should encourage those you minister to. Like Abraham, you are called to be blessed and to be a blessing to others (see Gen. 12:2). Ask yourself this question: "Is this word encouraging? Will it bless the one I'm ministering to? Will it build them up or bring comfort?"

It does not conflict with the Scriptures. John 17:17 states that a true inspired word from God will never violate the counsel of the Scriptures. Always search the Bible in order to support your revelation.

It represents God's nature. First Corinthians 13 shows God's nature to be loving, kind, and merciful; He is full of truth and righteousness. Since they represent the Author, true prophetic words will never be rude, distasteful, judgmental, critical, boastful, or corrupt. They will always represent the heart of God's saving grace as "the testimony of Jesus is the spirit of prophecy" (Rev. 19:10). Jesus means "Savior," and the spirit of prophecy represents His saving nature.

It bears witness. Most often, a true prophetic word will bear witness in a person's heart, although sometimes a person might not understand the word right away.

It is often confirmed by outward circumstances. When you speak a word over someone, he or she can usually confirm it through situations that are happening in his or her life.

Does it come to pass? If a prophetic word has a foretelling dimension, then, of course, its fulfillment is the ultimate proof.

GROWING IN THE PROPHETIC

Practice makes perfect, so take every opportunity to prophesy. You will get more proficient in the gift by using it more. You become a better prayer warrior not by attending more prayer seminars, but by doing more praying. With every skill in life, practice makes perfect. This principle is also true of the prophetic and of evangelism. Faith without works is dead, so activate the prophetic by faith. Practice the gift.

Journaling will help you mature in your prophetic gift. Write out what you believe the Lord is saying and then verify it by studying out the Scriptures. Look back over your journal and meditate on what the Lord has revealed to you.

Good accountability is important. Make sure you are submitted to spiritual authorities and mature peers who can speak into your life.

Make wrongs right. If you make a mistake, humble yourself and don't operate in an attitude of self-protection.

Overcome Jezebel. Jezebel is an evil spirit that attacks the prophetic gift. Most often, Jezebel uses intimidating thoughts and accusations to assault those stepping out in faith. Don't allow intimidation to hold you back.

Carol Arnott, of the Toronto Airport Christian Fellowship, once explained to our team that she didn't like the term "prophetic evangelism." She said that the phrase was intimidating and caused her to feel as if she needed to operate in some special power before being able to reach out to others. What follows is an interview that she gave our team. I believe that Carol's words will encourage you:

> God loves everyone. It's just that simple. He is intensely interested in each and every person, whether they're a Christian or not. It's so important for unbelievers to hear that God truly cares about them. Everyone needs to know that He is a God of love, and not a God who is easily given to anger or judgment. Even in some of the terrible and harmful things that souls engage in, God is still full of love and compassion and desires to reach out to deliver and heal! And when the lost realize that He cares and loves them just as they are, it changes their whole life.

There are many ways to reach those who don't know the Lord, but what better way for them to experience His love than to hear His words of encouragement? I think this is what is so exciting about prophetic evangelism. We have lots of prophetic encouragement flowing in the Church, but we need to take it into the streets and the marketplace. There are individuals in our church who have been going to the streets and ministering to unbelievers with prophetic words of encouragement on a regular basis. The testimonies have been outstanding. The unsaved are actually longing for anointed destiny words. We are called to answer that longing.

Many believers, however, are intimidated by the term "prophet" or "prophetic." They feel that to operate in any level of prophetic expression there needs to be some kind of special touch on their lives. This is not true, of course, if you have Christ in your heart. Although we might not all be called to a prophetic office, every believer can hear the voice of God and share His inspired words of love and encouragement. Don't let yourself get tangled up in terms or images or expectations. I personally like to forget about being "prophetic" and just focus on being intimate with the Lord. If you do that, if you just focus on connecting with Him, prophetic words come naturally, and so does reaching the lost. It all flows from intimacy. When we are intimate with our Father, there is no fear, no sense of must-do; there's just joy and love.

For me, "prophetic evangelism" can be a scary term. I often feel pressured at the thought of having to cough up a prophetic word on the streets. I prefer to just take Daddy by the hand and follow His leading each day. If I walk close with Him, I will understand

His heart. I will then hear His words, and that's what being prophetic is all about. When we are intimate with the Lord, people will be drawn to Him. It is His presence of love that draws. If we focus on terms like "prophetic evangelism," it can make us choke up and be nervous. If we focus on Him, though, it's easy. It is simply understanding that He is always with us and will give us what we need to bless another person. It's not about us and what we have to do; it's about Him and what He longs to do through us.

When I approach someone to share the gospel, I know He'll be there. When I pray for the sick, He'll be there. When I need to give a prophetic encouragement, I am confident that He is there to give me the inspiration. In the same way that He is with me in my prayer and soaking times, He is with me everywhere I go and in everything I do. His presence is always there. It is just so fun holding on to Father's hand and watching Him move.

WAYS TO EXPRESS THE PROPHETIC

The prophetic gift is simply one way of manifesting God's love, and there are many ways of expressing the prophetic in evangelism. Be creative! Take His hand and see where and how He leads you. Not only can you speak prophetic words, but you can write them out, draw them out, dance them out, and express them through musical instruments and lyrics. You can minister the words to those in churches, restaurants, public transport systems, street corners, workplaces, schools, and homes. Anywhere there are people, you can prophesy as the Holy Spirit directs.

If you have the Holy Spirit dwelling within you, you can prophesy! Remember it's easy! The lost are waiting to be encouraged and blessed. Dry bones are waiting to come to life. Darkness is waiting to receive light. Prophesy! You can do it!

6

CHAPTER

Starting a
Goodness Revolution

...HOW GOD ANOINTED JESUS OF NAZARETH
WITH THE HOLY SPIRIT AND POWER AND HOW
HE WENT AROUND DOING GOOD AND HEAL-
ING ALL WHO WERE UNDER THE POWER OF
THE DEVIL, BECAUSE GOD WAS WITH HIM
(ACTS 10:38).

Previous chapters discussed the power of God available to
His children to work miracles and move in the prophetic. God
is leading His Church in the direction of moving in the supernatural realm. Although this is true, and we will definitely see
darkness invaded with miraculous light, yet another dimension
exists as regards Christ's anointing and power. Jesus was
anointed with the Holy Spirit and with power. What was this
anointing and power for? What effect did it have? Acts 10:38
says that by the anointing and power of the Spirit, Jesus went
about "doing good." God's anointing and power prepares us to
engage in *good* works just as Jesus did.

God is a *good* God, and we are called to preach good
news. Everything about His nature and Kingdom is *good!*

Believers are to carry this goodness into the darkness. You may be reading this book and think, "Oh my, I could never prophesy or work miracles!" Perhaps you are not yet ready to step into that realm, but everyone can do acts of goodness under the Spirit's anointing. You can use the same power that graced Jesus to engage in good works. Sometimes, the simplest act done in love and faith can work a mighty miracle of salvation.

A LOAF OF BREAD AND A NOTE

Many people in the world have never known a simple act of kindness. Years ago, I remember hosting a children's Bible club when our sons were young. We invited all the children from our neighborhood. Two brothers living a few houses down from us attended and received a powerful touch from the Lord. As a result, they received Christ. Previously I had noticed that the curtains on their house were always drawn, and I never saw their mother. Rumor had it that she was involved in witch-craft. The boys informed me that their mother suffered with depression and didn't go out very much.

While making bread for our family one day, I noticed that I had enough dough for five loaves instead of my usual four. Sensing that the Lord wanted to bless the boys' mother, I wrapped up the extra loaf and wrote a little note that said, "Jesus loves you. Have a good day!" That afternoon, the boys took home the wrapped loaf of bread and note to their mother.

A number of months later, I found myself praying daily for this woman. Her children regularly attended Sunday school with us, but we never heard from the mother and she never answered the phone when we called. One day, I felt impressed to go to her home and invite myself in for a visit. After ringing the doorbell a few times, the door opened just a crack and a woman's head peeked out of the opening. I introduced myself, and asked if I could come in for a visit. She replied with a monotone voice and pronounced each syllable methodically, "It would be better if I came to your house." I responded that I would be delighted to have her come to my home. The boys' mother told me that she would meet me there in about 15 minutes.

Sure enough, 15 minutes later, she rang our doorbell. Opening the door, I saw a woman with an almost frightful appearance. Her dyed, jet-black hair, white pasty face, glazed-over eyes, frail body, and deep monotone voice all presented an air of death and hopelessness. Completely black attire accentuated the woman's rather morbid look.

We shared coffee together. At first, the conversation was a bit uncomfortable. She would answer my questions with one-word answers and add nothing to enhance the communication. Not only that, she stared at the wall the entire time. After what seemed a long while, she opened up and shared all her emotional pain. Due to depression, she had not left her house for two years, and a problem with alcoholism in the home also made matters difficult. This woman was clothed in shame and worthlessness.

I shared the gospel and invited her to receive Christ. She did, and even cracked a little smile. For a second, she managed to look into my eyes. Lifting her shaky little hand, she reached into her black purse. After shuffling around in it for a moment, she pulled out a little note. "I don't know if you remember this or not," she said, "but a number of months ago you gave me a loaf of bread with this little note. It was the only time I can ever remember someone saying that I was loved. Every day, I read this note—it means so much to me. Thank you, for being so kind."

That little act of goodness had opened her heart to the gospel. She went on to become a regular church member and her life got better and happier. She often reminded me of the loaf of bread and the kind note that led her to a complete change. Her life with God became a major influence on her entire family. "The goodness of God [which] leads you to repentance" (Rom. 2:4, NKJ).

STARTING A GOODNESS REVOLUTION

Graham Cooke once said, "The problem with the world isn't that there is too much corruption, violence, immorality, or perversion. The problem is that there is not enough goodness." He explained how his church in England took on a neighborhood as a project and, each day, engaged in acts of goodness. They mowed lawns, washed windows, took dogs for walks, and drove folks to doctor's appointments or grocery shopping. They simply found out what people's needs were and then met them. As a result, the neighborhood's spiritual climate drastically changed; everyone was happier, friendlier, and some came to Christ. The "goodness team" caused a positive reaction.

Engaging in acts of goodness not only benefits the one receiving the blessing, but it leaves you feeling really good too. It's a win-win situation. Everyone gets blessed! Graham's suggestion triggered the vision in me that starting a goodness revolution would be quite easy. If the Body of Christ used the anointing to simply do acts of goodness, we could change the spiritual climate of our cities.

Fear dissipates in the presence of goodness, and cruelty loses its power and influence. Jesus taught us to fight evil with good. Goodness is a powerful force. Priests at the dedication of Solomon's temple (see 2 Chron. 7) could not enter inside because the Lord's glorious presence so filled the room. Seeing fire flash down from Heaven and a temple full of glory, the people fell to the ground and praised God: "He is good; His love endures forever" (2 Chron. 7:3).

After Graham's word, I suggested that our team should launch a goodness revolution. The whole event ended up being so much fun! That particular summer, 12 members of our team lived together in the same house for over three months. Now, such a set-up definitely has some potential for fallout! We committed to focusing on living in an environment of goodness, which turned out to be infectious. When one person starts, then others respond in like manner. We would say things like, "I'm going to help you with the dishes, even though it's not my assignment, because I am working on a goodness revolution." Then someone would respond, "No, it's okay. I want to bless you! You go rest and let *me* do the dishes." Another person would come in and say, "Hey, why don't we all do it together because I want to help, too."

We had daily contests for who would go get coffee treats for everyone, because so many wanted to "treat." As was often the case, a number of them ended up going out together to get treats. We cut the neighbors' lawns, made grocery hampers for those in need, and helped people at the supermarkets take groceries to the car. Everyone had fun as we worked on it together. I firmly believe that spiritual and relational environments in homes and families can change dramatically if everyone gets committed to launching a goodness revolution. After that, take it to the neighbors, the workplace, church, and school. Once the "movement" begins, then everyone will jump on board.

DEFINING A GOODNESS REVOLUTION

Let's look at definitions and synonyms of the words *goodness* and *revolution*. Then apply these concepts to your imagination as you ponder what a goodness revolution might look like in your home and community. *Goodness* is "the state or quality of being good, upright, honorable, charitable, moral, righteous, considerate, tolerant, generous, kind, agreeable, pleasant, and genuine." *Revolution* is "a complete or radical change of any kind."

You don't need too much spiritual discernment to discover the need for such a revolution in today's world. People are often uncaring and thoughtless of others. Imagine a radical change in your sphere of influence. Instead of cruel words, kind words would be spoken. Instead of immorality, purity would prevail. Instead of violence, gentleness would be shown. Instead of greed and selfishness, generosity would be lavished on others. Goodness is a powerful force that can change the world!

Many people do not feel comfortable engaging in aggressive power or prophetic evangelism, but everyone can do acts of kindness under the Spirit's anointing. More goodness shown in homes and communities would result in less divorce, less sibling rivalry, less crime, less insecurity, and a lot less rebellion. Goodness is a great way of penetrating darkness with light. Many more would come to Christ as we represented Him correctly. After all, He is a good God!

A SIMPLE SMILE THAT SPOKE DESTINY

Recently, while ministering on the streets, I met a wonderful woman of God whom I will call *Anne*. Not yet 30 years old, she has only been saved a few years out of a life of prostitution. She grew up in a very difficult home situation and was placed in many different foster homes as a young girl. Some were healthy and loving households, but others were anything but that. While only 12 years old, she ran away from an abusive foster care environment and became trapped in a life of prostitution and drug addiction. Before she turned 13, she started selling her body in the slums of a large North American city.

From that moment on, Anne stepped into the darkest years of her life.

For more than 12 years, she worked as a street prostitute. In all that time, she claimed that not one person ever spoke anything to her that could pass for a word of kindness, affirmation, or value. No one showed her acts of goodness, care, and love. Not even one person. Not even one time. Anne gave birth to three children. While she was out turning tricks and scoring drugs, no one ever reached out to help the kids. She tried her best to care for them, but admits that her best was not very good at all. Anne often locked them up in the house alone, while she prostituted herself to make money for her drug habit. She lived in constant fear that the social services would discover her neglectful treatment of the children, yet she was imprisoned by her lifestyle and addiction, unable to change through her own strength.

Life was a vicious cycle of pain, hopelessness, and despair, and she saw no way out. Anne explained, "When you work the streets, everyone thinks you're trash and they make you feel that way too. You can hear it in their voice. You can see it in their eyes." Her life was constantly in danger. Anne couldn't even count the number of times she found herself in the jaws of death. Somehow, she was always mysteriously protected and preserved.

One day, a young woman walked by Anne on the street. She stopped momentarily and looked into Anne's eyes. Anne doesn't remember the woman saying anything, but she does recall that this woman smiled the warmest, most accepting smile she had ever seen. Anne said it felt like liquid love, and that acceptance was being poured into her. Anne stood speechless. For the first time in years, she felt clean and valued, as if something inside her had finally awoken after a long sleep. The young woman who took a moment to cast that special smile was a Christian. She planted a seed of

Jesus' love that reconnected Anne with her destiny and value as a human being.

Anne did not get born again that day, but she was deeply touched through an act of goodness. The love of God had soothed her wounded heart and she would never be the same. A few days later, Anne met another believer who saw beyond her current state and felt compassion for her. Willing to step out in faith, this Christian woman offered to help Anne financially, if she would leave a life of prostitution. Anne could barely believe what she heard. So, she accepted the offer and promised to stop turning tricks, but did not yet make a commitment to come off drugs.

That believer belonged to an entire church community that rallied around Anne. They became involved in her recovery and in her life. That commitment turned out to be huge, as Anne had to be taught almost everything about living a life off the streets. She had never learned how to cook meals, clean a home, care for children, or organize household affairs. Even though Anne was now in her mid-20s, she had to be trained in the basics. Her new church family helped her with all these needs. They supported her with finances, prayer, and all sorts of practical help. They took her shopping for food, cared for her children, took her to doctor's appointments, and taught her parenting skills and how to clean and keep a home. They stood with her through every trial, which wasn't always easy. Even in the many testing times, they literally came alongside of Anne and pulled her out of darkness. God's goodness truly lifted her out of the mire.

Every day, Anne saw the love of Jesus through these people and their kindness. She gave her heart to the Lord. A short time following her deliverance from the streets, Anne signed herself into a drug rehab program. For several years, she has been clean of drug use and free from a life of prostitution.

She's a great mom who loves and cares for her children well, and she shines for Jesus with a glow that is indescribable.

Anne is walking the streets again. But now she does so as an ambassador of the Kingdom, who shares her testimony of Christ's transforming love. This is the power of the gospel, which is the same today as it was 2,000 years ago. His love never lost its power. All we need to do is embrace that love and walk out its promises. Anne's life was transformed by the love of Jesus. Just think, it all began with a simple act of goodness—a God-filled smile that said, "You have value; you have worth; your life counts; you are beautiful and altogether lovely." The smile that spoke destiny into her life was actually a prophetic smile of evangelism.

To see a simple act of goodness bear such fruit is amazing. That initial "smile connection" didn't take much time or involve any financial or relational commitment. Yet, something so simple managed to bring such huge influence. We can all smile. So, why not find someone to smile at today and begin a goodness revolution in someone's life.

I deeply admire and respect the church body that reached out to Anne. They stepped up to the plate and operated in love, patience, sacrifice, and goodness in ways that few would dare to. I can just imagine them standing before the Lord in the final day as He proclaims over them with deep delight in His heart, "Well done, you good and faithful servants!"

LET YOUR LIGHT SHINE

Jesus said, "In the same way, let your light shine before men, that they may see your good deeds and praise your Father in heaven" (Matt. 5:16). At times, we are not to let our right hand know what the left hand is doing as we engage in "secret acts of kindness." But there are also moments when the Holy Spirit will deliberately call us to publicly display our good deeds. Such exposure is not for personal glory, but for that of the Father.

We have heard testimonies of many Christians who have aggressively made strategies to implement acts of goodness as part of an outreach. Such examples are always refreshing to see! Some have given out free iced soda on hot days or hot chocolate on cold nights. Others have made food hampers for the poor, and visited lonely, elderly residents in nursing homes. Many have taken in foster children. Youth groups have done clean-up jobs in neighborhoods and given free washes for cars and windshields. Others have given generously of their finances. The heart of God holds many creative ideas.

Why not pray about how you can begin a goodness revolution in your home, family, and community? Make goodness a lifestyle and, remember, you reap what you sow! Do you know what that means? If you sow generously of your time, resources, and gifts, then you are in for a great life filled with a bountiful return of goodness! Being good is really good, and now is a great time to bring light into the darkness.

7

CHAPTER

The Message

FOR GOD SO LOVED THE WORLD THAT HE
GAVE HIS ONE AND ONLY SON, THAT WHOEVER
BELIEVES IN HIM SHALL NOT PERISH BUT HAVE
ETERNAL LIFE (JOHN 3:16).

If believers are going to bring light into darkness, then we need to understand the message of the gospel of love. The key to seeing a soul come to Christ is not found in a technique or an evangelistic program, but rather in a revelation of Jesus Christ, Savior of the world. I am amazed at how many Christians do not understand the message of the Cross or the eternal, unbreakable, love covenant that God secured for mankind through Christ. Understanding this very message is crucial to bringing light into darkness. Once that revelation is received, sharing the message with others is easy and we will see the Kingdom advance.

When Jesus came to the region of Caesarea Philippi, He asked His disciples, "Who do people say the Son of Man is?"...Simon Peter answered, "You are the Christ, the Son of the living God." Jesus replied, "Blessed are you, Simon son of Jonah, for this was not revealed to you by man, but

by My Father in heaven. And I tell you that...on this rock
[the revelation] I will build My church, and the gates of
Hades will not overcome it" (Matthew 16:13, 16-18).

The gospel message is the message of love in its purest
form—it is the revelation of Christ, God's gift to mankind.
"Behold what manner of love the Father has bestowed on us
that we should be called children of God" (1 John 3:1, NKJ). What
manner of love would motivate a perfect, holy, and righteous
God to offer a sinful and rebellious person the right to become
His very own dear child and heir of all that He is and has? This
sounds like an extravagant act, doesn't it? Indeed, this is the
very manner of love shown by the Father to each and every one
of us. Nothing throughout all mankind's history has ever
prompted Him to withdraw this love, even though we have all
continually put His love to the test. His demonstration of love
does not change because He is unchangeable.

GOD WANTED A FAMILY

God desired children, and everyone ever born was
desired by God. No one was a mistake. Everyone has value
and purpose. God is love, and the nature of love gives and lav-
ishes goodness and kindness on others. God desired a family
so that He could lavish His love on each and every one; this is
His nature.

In the beginning, God created trees, flowers, birds, fish,
animals, and a host of other earthly and celestial creations. He
loved everything He created and, each day, He said, "It is
good." Even though He was very pleased, He still longed for a
precious creation made in His likeness—an object of affection
to fulfill the longing of His righteous heart.

In our first year of marriage, my husband Ron and I did
not have children. We did, however, have two dogs. Although
we enjoyed our dogs and they were like family, they did not

satisfy our longing for children. The dogs were nice, but not *that* nice. Something inside us said, "Children, children, children." That longing was a small taste of what the Lord felt in His heart for mankind. Dogs and other creatures were not enough for Him either. Although He took pleasure in them, they did not satisfy His desire for children made in His own image and likeness.

God deeply desired children, yet even before man was created, He knew we were going to cause Him great pain. As a result of foreknowing our sinful failures, He initiated a plan to rescue our lives from the power of sin. In the Bible, this act is called "redemption." He actually took care of the problem for us before we even acted out the problem. (The Lamb *was* slain *before* the foundation of the world, as stated in Revelation 13:8). God has never been caught off guard by mankind's failures!

Years ago, I said to the Lord, "I wouldn't choose to have children if I knew ahead of time they were going to rebel, betray, and dishonor me. I would be much happier without that type of child! Why then did You create us?"

In response, He spoke this clear word, "My plan was to prove to mankind that My love would withstand every resistance. I allowed My love to be tested so that you would know it would always stand and never be withdrawn. I am Love. When anyone chooses through an act of their free will to come into relationship with Me, they will never, ever need to doubt My love for them. Knowing I passed every test, they will feel completely secure and that is My desire." That's how much He loves you. Isn't that amazing? Behold what manner of love is this?

THE CROSS AND THE COVENANT

God's plan for mankind is to have an eternal relationship established through a covenant, which is a legally binding agreement between two people or parties. For a covenant to work, there must be absolute integrity in its making and in keeping all terms. Entering a covenant with a person of integrity gives a sense of protection and security. That's what the marriage covenant is supposed to be like. The vow to be faithful, to care for and to honor each other, should give a sense of belonging and oneness with a covenant partner. The purpose of covenant is to legally secure a relationship.

Mankind does not have a history of being good covenant keepers, so what *should* offer security (the marriage covenant) makes many people feel insecure. Some don't even bother getting married anymore because they think, *It might last or it might not.* That is one reason why so much family breakdown occurs nowadays. Broken covenants are everywhere, as evidenced by the high divorce rate in our nation. God, however, is a covenant-keeping God. He is full of integrity and always keeps the terms of the covenants He makes.

The original meaning of the word *covenant* was "where the blood flows." Ancient covenants always set terms and exchanged names, weapons, and resources. Almost always, these covenants included a consummation ceremony through the mingling of blood. At the end of the ceremony, a covenant meal was served to celebrate this union. A marriage covenant is a blood covenant in a similar manner. We make our vows before witnesses (an exchanging of terms), we exchange names (the bride usually takes her husband's name), and we exchange resources (in most cases, the assets of one legally become that of the other). The marriage is then consummated through the sexual act, which breaks the woman's hymen membrane (the shedding of blood).

God's covenant plan for His relationship with man was a blood covenant (Christ's blood shed for us at the Cross). He set the terms (through the Old Testament law and prophets) and then defined a name exchange (Jesus said, "In My *name,* ask..."), a weapons exchange (Jesus' weapons and armor are ours), and a resource exchange (He became poor that we might become rich). In ancient civilizations, a representative of one tribe would cut covenant with a representative of another tribe. When the two leaders cut covenant on behalf of their peoples, both tribes enjoyed the benefits of covenant. Christ did the same for us when He represented mankind in a covenant with God. Jesus was, and is, our covenant representative and leader. As our covenant representative, His responsibility is to keep all terms for us. In exchange, we receive all the covenant blessings. Wow!

THE AMAZING GOOD NEWS

God desired to make a covenant with mankind that would secure us in relationship with Him for all eternity. He knew, however, that once we fell into sin, we would never be able to keep covenant. Humans were now filled with a sin nature, which made it impossible for us to hold up our end of the agreement. To fulfill the covenant terms, God required a sinless representative for mankind who would keep all the conditions. But no sinless person could be found. As a result He chose to fill this position Himself. By becoming a man, He took our place in covenant. Jesus also took God's place in covenant— because He is God. He is both Man and God; in reality then, He was cutting covenant with Himself. This is how God could cut an eternal, unbreakable, unfailing covenant with humans. To fulfill this plan, Jesus, who was fully God, left Heaven and came into the sinful world as a man.

When He came as a man, He had to fulfill all of man's covenant terms as laid out in Old Testament law. If He failed to fulfill every point of the law, or if He gave in to temptation just once, then He would not qualify as a keeper of covenant on mankind's behalf. Though that would have been devastating for us, He had an even greater risk. In Scripture, Jesus is referred to as "the last Adam" (1 Cor. 15:45). The first Adam was a perfect man before the Fall; he was made in God's image and likeness. When he fell into temptation, the rule and dominion that God had given him was surrendered to satan. Romans 6:16 teaches that submitting ourselves to sin turns us into sin's slave. Adam became such a slave when he submitted to satan's temptation, and that also would have happened to the last Adam (Jesus), if He had fallen into even the slightest temptation. Only pure Love would be willing to take a risk like that.

JESUS THE MAN

Jesus came just as the first Adam did. He was of mankind's nature, yet without sin. He was to fulfill man's requirement in covenant with human power and capabilities. The Holy Spirit came upon Him to empower Him, just as the Holy Spirit empowers you today. Through the Holy Spirit's power, Jesus the Man remained sinless throughout His entire life on the earth. You need to understand that He resisted sin in *man's* strength, with the power of the Holy Spirit helping Him. Even though Jesus was perfect and without a sin nature, He had a huge wrestle in His soul against sin.

Jesus had to wrestle to secure the victory as a man so as to restore mankind's rightful place in relationship with God, like the first Adam had before the fall. Ultimately, at the end of His "covenant course," Jesus Christ would be acknowledged as a perfect God *and* a perfect Man who would sit on a throne at God's right hand. He would ultimately sum up all things in Heaven and in earth.

Christ did not have an easy time resisting sin. At one point, He found resisting temptation to be so grueling that He sweat drops of blood (see Heb. 12:4). Jesus did it in man's power for all of us, so we wouldn't have to in our own strength—because we couldn't. Everything required for mankind to enter covenant with God was fulfilled through the Man, Jesus Christ. He fulfilled all the law and the prophets.

JESUS COUNTS THE COST

Before the foundation of the world, Jesus probably had to ask Himself, "How big is My love? Am I willing to perform acts of love, kindness, and mercy for people who don't even desire Me? Am I able to love so deeply that I would actually become sin for those whom I love? Am I willing to taste death and pay the penalty of sin for those who hate and despise Me?" He counted the cost and, with all of us in mind, made a love choice, saying, "Oh, yes! You are worth everything to Me. I will gladly leave Heaven and pay the price with joy."

JESUS ARRIVES ON EARTH

Mary conceived Jesus by the power of the Holy Spirit. She and Joseph traveled to Bethlehem where she went into labor. No lodging was available, so Mary gave birth in an animal stable and laid baby Jesus in a feeding trough. What type of treatment was this for man's Savior? No palace, no special treatment, and hardly anyone even discerned who He was. Right away, Jesus had to start passing love tests. If He had been offended, He could have thought, *Well, that's it, I'm going back to Heaven. I tried to do something nice for you, but you treated Me like an animal and threw Me in a feeding trough.* Jesus, however, did not take offense, but passed the love test in tremendous humility. Even though He was worthy of the most extravagant treatment, He didn't demand or expect it. He came to serve.

King Herod even tried to have Him killed as a baby, but Jesus never stopped loving. He never withdrew love and never lost faith. What would you do if your only motivation was to help people and, all of a sudden, they're trying to kill you? You'd probably say something like, "I don't need you. I'll go somewhere else." But Jesus had a different heart.

HIS MINISTRY BEGINS

Jesus taught in the synagogues as a rabbi. The religious leaders examined His teachings carefully. They knew the Scriptures and were considered experts in the Word of God and doctrine. Jesus, however, *is* true doctrine; He *is* the living Word; He *is* true theology and yet these very leaders called Him a blasphemer and a heretic. The religious leaders attempted to bring legal charges against Him. This is how they treated the true God. How would you feel if you were God? There you are, teaching truth right from Heaven. You're speaking truth, because you *are* Truth, and the people you came to save are saying, "You're a liar, a deceiver, a heretic and you're teaching us false doctrine. You're demonized." Character assaults like this are much worse than simply saying, "Your theology is off."

I've experienced a little of that resistance myself, and I must say that those times were brutal. Everything in me wanted to withdraw. Jesus, however, never withdrew love or Himself from us, not for one single moment. Each time He was opposed or mistreated by man, His love once again passed the test. He said, "I will never withdraw love and I will never lose faith." Through all the mistreatment, He kept consistent in love and faith.

Jesus chose 12 disciples and then 70 more, and He poured His time and life into them by giving, teaching, and mentoring them day in and day out. Many others also followed His ministry. His own followers didn't always treat Him well, but with all the disappointments He suffered, He never wavered in His commitment to them.

THE GARDEN OF GETHSEMANE

One of Christ's most excruciating struggles was in Gethsemane (which means "the oil press"). He faced every temptation that man would ever encounter. Strong forces of hell were spiritually assaulting Him. As we established earlier, Jesus had to resist sin as a man—in the same strength as the first Adam. The entire time He was wrestling against temptation, we were in His heart. The pressure against His soul was so great that He sweat blood in His resistance to sin. With every drop of blood that pushed through His bursting capillaries, He was saying, "For you, I will resist. No matter what it feels like. No matter how excruciating it is. My emotions are being wrung out beyond explanation, but it's all for you."

I've personally faced some grueling spiritual battles and have been assaulted by some powerful demonic entities. Although these seasons were unbearably painful, they were nothing at all in comparison to what Jesus experienced. I am a little aware, however, of the crushing feeling that pressures your emotions and mind during such times. In the midst of such a battle, it is essential to keep focused because all you have is the Word of God to stand on. Everything else going on in your life seems contrary to the Truth, but there's just one point of choice: "I will stand on Your Word, Lord, no matter what. I will trust my soul into Your keeping." At the end of these battles, your emotions, thought processes, and even physical body are weakened, fatigued, and fragile. The impact of such warfare is very excruciating, and no words can describe it. What any of us could experience in this level of warfare, however, is still nothing in comparison to the pressure experienced by Jesus.

What was it like for Jesus when the hordes of hell were trying to take Him out? What motivated Him to stand through this agony? God didn't need to put Himself in this position. Do you know why He did? Because of His love for you and all mankind, no matter how sinful we are. He said, "I'm doing this to fulfill your covenant requirements." He loves us that much. For just a moment, forget about everyone else on the face of the earth. If you alone were left, He'd do it just for you. In the midst of Gethsemane's agony, *you* were in His vision. The thought of having us with Him for all eternity was His motivation to continue. Our faces gave Him the strength to endure.

BETRAYED, ABANDONED, DENIED

Jesus departed from the garden in a weak and exhausted state. Judas, one of the twelve disciples, approached Him, and betrayed Him with a kiss. Even though Jesus knew Judas would betray Him, He continued to call him *friend*. He said, "*Friend*, do what you came for" (Matt. 26:50). Betrayal is very painful. If you have been betrayed, you know how difficult this is on your emotions. But even betrayal could not make Jesus withdraw love or friendship. I can't imagine being in a ferocious spiritual battle and then having to experience betrayal by a dear friend and coworker in the next moment. To accentuate the pain even more, all of His closest followers and friends fled from Him at His arrest.

When you're in a hard place, being falsely accused, you just want someone—even if it's only one person—to stand with you. *Is there one who will just come to My side right now? Is there one who will believe in Me? Is there one who will defend Me?* Jesus did not even have one. His own disciples, whom He had poured into for three years, all fled in fear of their reputation. As Jesus was led away, He heard one of His closest disciples, Peter, swearing, "No, I never knew Him." Oh, how painful it must have been for Jesus to hear that denial. He knew prophetically that Peter would do this, but foreknowledge doesn't ease the emotional devastation when betrayal actually happens.

HIS TRIAL

False witnesses were paid to testify against Jesus in court. That is harsh! When you know someone is lying about you, the natural tendency is to immediately defend yourself. Isaiah 53:7 reveals, "He was oppressed and afflicted, yet He did not open

His mouth; He was led like a lamb to the slaughter, and as a sheep before her shearers is silent, so He did not open His mouth." He had purposed in His heart to offer unconditional love and mercy toward the lying witnesses. He must have thought, *You can line your pockets with filthy lucre, but you cannot make Me withdraw My love from you.*

They stripped Him naked, placed a crown of thorns on His head, and mocked Him openly. Even though you and I were not yet created, we were hidden there in the heart of depraved humanity. We might believe that we would never hurt or deny Him, but, like Peter, we may not understand the weakness of our own flesh. Probably, each of us would have acted in the same way. Christ's love was being severely tested by mankind. We have put His love to the test many times, yet He has never abandoned us or withdrawn love, and He never will.

BEATEN AND SCOURGED

Jesus was beaten, spit upon, and mocked. His face was violently struck, apparently to the point of making Him unrecognizable. Again, with every cruel punch, His response was only love as He gazed into the eyes of His tormentors. He was brutally scourged with a whip of nine leather strips. Little pieces of sharp metal or bone sat at the end of each strip. Each stroke provided nine lashings. A common belief held that 40 lashes would bring death. Under Roman laws, He might have received even more than that. History reveals that His flesh was literally ripped open, exposing His innards. Every time the whip's razor-sharp edge dug into His flesh, we were in His heart. We were the reason He could endure such hostility. Looking into the faces of those cruelly scourging Him, He would have once again said, "You cannot make Me withdraw My love." He would have assured us of that today as well, if our hand were holding the scourge.

CRUCIFIED

Jesus carried a heavy wooden cross that was heaved onto His back. Weakened with pain, He staggered up Calvary's hill. An angry mob followed Him, mocking, ridiculing, and shouting, "Crucify Him! Crucify Him!" They nailed His hands and feet to the cross and hung Him between two guilty criminals. An innocent man was being crucified.

To many, it appeared that Jesus was defeated and that He was being *taken*, but, in actuality, His existence was being *given*. The devil, the false witnesses, the Romans, the Jews, or any other man or woman did not take Jesus' life. He freely gave His life. When you see Jesus hanging on the Cross, you see love Himself hanging there. He, as a free gift of love, had been completely proven and tested against everything that could possibly oppose or destroy it.

Love Himself was on that Cross, stripped naked and humiliated, hanging there in agonizing pain. Amidst all his agony, one of the thieves asked to be saved. Jesus didn't hesitate. In His own greatest point of need, He continued to pour Himself out. He could have said, "What do you mean you want a favor from Me? I don't deserve to be here, and you do. Forget about it; it's too late!" But Jesus wasn't and isn't like that. He proved His love once again, "Of course, I will save you. In fact, today I'll do it and you will be with Me in paradise. You will see the glory of My salvation."

Looking down from His cross, Jesus saw a mass of people—a crowd who delighted to watch Him die. The chief priests and teachers cried out, "…He can't save Himself. Let this Christ, this king of Israel, come down now from the cross, that we may see and believe" (Mark 15:31-32). His merciful, loving retaliation to the taunting crowd was, "Father, forgive them for they do not know what they are doing" (Luke 23:34). Can you imagine that? We sometimes find it difficult to forgive those who hurt or offend us. Consider Jesus: A mass of angry people rallied against Him, and we were there too—all of humanity stood there. Oh yes, He saw our faces in the crowd that day. We all sinned against Him and yet He said, "Father, forgive them all." Right at that point, He forgave all the sins of mankind. He canceled the debt of sin. Only pure Love Himself could do that.

Jesus went even further and actually chose to become mankind's sin. He chose to have our sin poured into Him, so that He could pour His righteousness into us. Jesus chose to become something abhorrent that would be judged, so that we would be free from judgment. Have you ever been mistreated, taken advantage of, or sinned against? Doesn't seeing the offender punished give you a great feeling, knowing that the discipline is what is deserved? But Jesus' heart was different. He said, "No, I'll take the punishment for your sin. I'll take full responsibility. You can go free."

A number of years ago I was on the mission field, and I misjudged a particular situation and, consequently, made some bad decisions. My actions seriously hurt some individuals. When I finally saw the situation clearly, I was terribly grieved, overwhelmed, and deeply ashamed. I thought, *I should have known better, and I shouldn't have done that.* I had difficulty believing that I hadn't seen the situation through eyes of wisdom in the first place. I asked for forgiveness from one individual who was particularly wounded through the process. The person refused to extend the undeserved mercy that I desperately needed. For years afterwards, I had a very difficult time forgiving myself.

One day, I cried out to the Lord in prayer, "Don't let my failure continue to hurt them. Don't let it ruin their lives." I felt terrible to the very core of my being. The Lord spoke very soberly to me, "You didn't commit that sin. You didn't make that mistake. I did." Surprised, I said, "What? No,

Lord! You never did that. I'm the one who did it." But He insisted, "I did it." Again, I persisted to defend His innocence, "Jesus, no, You didn't. You are perfect and You have never wronged anyone, ever!"

He tenderly responded, "I bore your mistake on the Cross 2,000 years ago. I chose to take full responsibility for this mistake so that you might go free. I have even borne the judgment for it. You are free! I became this sin for you and, in exchange, I have given you My righteousness. This has all been paid in full. If there is any further problem, that hurting individual will need to come to Me. You have been totally released and fully justified. You never did it!"

I burst into tears of gratitude that flowed from deep inside my being. How could I not love a God who showed that much mercy? That day, He clearly revealed to me that this is what He's done for us all. This is what is called "substitution." He literally took our judgment and, in exchange, gave us His life and righteousness. Oh my, can we fully grasp this?

DYING IN FAITH

Gazing at all of us through the portals of time, Jesus died on the Cross in love and in faith. He "gave up the ghost" and cried out, "It is finished." Helpless, but remaining in faith, He entrusted His life into the hands of His Father. When Jesus became mankind's sin, He had no power to raise Himself from the dead. But God planned Christ's resurrection before the foundation of the world, and Jesus believed Him.

After His death, Jesus descended into the lower parts of the earth where He paid the full penalty for our sin. On the third day, His Heavenly Father raised Him from the dead. Following His resurrection, Mary and the other women, the disciples, and many others literally saw Jesus walking the earth. Oh yes, He is the Resurrection and the Life—the firstborn from the dead! When He was raised from the dead, He took the keys of death and hell. He stripped the devil of his authority and made an open show of him. Oh, what an eternal victory!

JESUS CHRIST IS FOREVER THE RESURRECTION AND THE LIFE

Through simply receiving Jesus as Savior by faith, everyone is invited into eternal relationship with God. All the work for mankind's redemption has been completed in Christ—it is finished! He cut an eternal, unbreakable covenant between God and man. In this covenant, He took the place of *both* man and God, which is why it can never be broken. The sinless, perfect Lamb of God has done everything for us. All we have left to do is simply believe.

Mankind's identity is found in Jesus, who accomplished everything for us. No man can boast in his own ability to save himself. Jesus fully paid a debt that we could never reimburse. All glory to Him! For forty days after His resurrection, Jesus walked the earth and then gloriously ascended to Heaven. He is forever seated at the right hand of God, "far above all principality and power and might and dominion and every name that is named…" (Eph. 1:20-21, NKJ). When we receive Him as our Savior, we are made to "sit together in the heavenly places in Christ Jesus" (Eph. 2:6, NKJ). Our lives are now "hidden with Christ in God" (Col. 3:3).

SEALED IN THE COVENANT

Everyone who believes in Christ has the gift of everlasting life and is forever sealed into a legally binding love agreement between God and man. This covenant is an eternal one that is impossible to break because it is between Jesus the Man and Jesus the God. Through His own sinless life, Jesus won our place for us. Believing in Him saves you from the separation from God created by sin. Your identity as a Kingdom child is not in your own ability to accomplish anything, but in His completed work. His ability is past tense—it is finished!

In fact, to be absolutely honest, right now, you are an utter failure outside of Christ. Pleasing God in your own strength is absolutely impossible! The only way anyone can please God is by believing in Christ. The arms of Jesus are open to all sinners. Simple faith connects believers to this glorious eternal salvation. All one needs to do is simply believe—that's it. "For it is by *grace* you have been saved, through faith—and this not from yourselves, it is the gift of God—not by works, so that no one can boast" (Eph. 2:8-9, emphasis own).

What is this *grace* that saves us? It is *His* divine influence in our lives. *He* chooses to accomplish everything for us. *His* work of favor is over us, and that is an undeserved, unmerited, favor. You, I, nor anyone else deserves it. His grace is His influence that comes upon our hearts and lives. We have been saved by grace through faith. That simple faith is what connects us to the glorious, finished work of the Cross. When, by faith, a person receives Jesus as personal Savior, His life enters their spirit. That individual is now, what the Scripture calls, *born again* (see John 3:1-9). They become a brand-new creation. Second Corinthians 5:17 (KJV) states, "Therefore if any man be in Christ, he is a new creature: old things are passed away; behold, all things are become new." Christ's brand-new life is inside that person, and His purity, love, peace, truth, and blessings now live within that human spirit. Faith saves an individual and faith keeps that person in Christ.

When an individual walks in true faith, they will live out the life of Christ that dwells within them. Their heart will love what the Father loves and will hate what He hates. Renewal will come to their minds and lives according to His righteousness and power. True faith in the finished work of the cross will lead a soul into true holiness. It is all in Christ. Without this faith, there is no salvation.

This is the glorious gospel that we preach. It is not a religious work, which pertains to man's attempts to please a holy God. The gospel is about Jesus Christ who is truly God and yet is fully Man. He is our identity. Christ is the Perfect Man who fulfilled all righteousness for us and He has invited all of His creation to come into Him. God longs to have an eternal love relationship with us and has made this possible through an eternal, unbreakable, blood covenant between Himself and Man. Jesus completed and fulfilled all the terms of the covenant for both God and Man and has invited the whole wide world into this glorious life.

> *For God so loved the world, that He gave His only begotten Son, that whoever believes in Him shall not perish but have eternal life. For God did not send the Son into the world to judge the world, but that the world might be saved through Him* (John 3:16-17, NAS).

Let's go now and proclaim this glorious gospel of the Kingdom to every creature. Let's take this message of light and life into the darkness.

8

CHAPTER

Making Disciples

GO THEREFORE AND MAKE DISCIPLES OF ALL NATIONS... (MATTHEW 28:19).

Just as a newborn needs nourishment and care, so do "new babes" in the Lord. God is calling His Body not only to preach the gospel, but also to disciple new believers. A new believer who gets fed and nurtured through loving Christian fellowship and the Word of God will grow strong in faith. A special call is now on the Body of Christ to disciple new believers.

A disciple is not only a believer, but also a devoted follower. Jesus gave the following command to His own disciples: "Therefore go and make disciples of all nations, baptizing them in the name of the Father and of the Son and of the Holy Spirit, and teaching them to obey everything I have commanded you. And surely I am with you always, to the very end of the age" (Matt. 28:19-20). These words differ from what He spoke in Mark 16:15: "Go into all the world and preach the good news to all creation." One command is to *preach* while the other is to *disciple*.

Some Christians believe that if you are not prepared to follow up with a new convert, then you shouldn't preach the gospel to them at all. Although seeing a new believer cared for is a noble desire, people *do* get saved through their faith in Jesus. Acts 2:21 says, "And everyone who calls on the name of the Lord will be saved." Romans 10:9-10 declares, "That if you confess with your mouth, 'Jesus is Lord,' and believe in your heart that God raised Him from the dead, you will be saved. For it is with your heart that you believe and are justified, and it is with your mouth that you confess and are saved." Furthermore, John 1:12 states, "Yet to all who received Him, to those who believed in His name, He gave the right to become children of God."

Salvation comes when people believe in Jesus and receive Him by faith into their hearts. It is a work of grace that requires a revelation, as in Matthew 16:16 when Peter declared Jesus Christ to be Son of the living God. In Romans 10:13-15, apostle Paul taught that everyone who calls upon the Lord's name shall be saved. But in order to believe, these people need to hear the gospel and that requires someone preaching to them. You and I can walk in this soul-winning anointing. Jesus has commissioned us to preach good news to the lost. The preached word releases a revelation of Christ that, in turn, births faith. When sharing the gospel, do so with the confidence that the Word will not return void but will accomplish everything it is sent to do (see Isa. 55:11).

In 1980, Ron, myself, and our children were on a three-month mission outreach in the inner city of Honolulu, Hawaii. Day and night we lived amongst the addicts, homeless, prostitutes, pimps, and criminals. We served, counseled, and helped them with personal affairs as well as took time to share Christ's life-giving message. But the people constantly disappointed us; they continually stole, lied, cheated, and manipulated. After the first month and a half, I began to harden my heart a bit. By the beginning of the third month, I had become intolerant.

Pouring out my complaint to the Lord, I said, "You might as well send us home! These people don't care about You. Look at them. We've shared the truth of the gospel over and over again with them and they are hardened. They don't care about You or us! Look, not one of them is saved as a result of all this time we have spent!" I continued to verbalize complaints rooted in self-pity and unrighteous indignation before the Lord.

He offered the firm, but loving, reply, "I never called you here to save these people!"

I cried out, "What? You didn't? Why are we here then? We gave up our home, our employment, and everything to win souls for You."

The Lord explained, "I have commissioned you to simply preach the gospel, not to save the lost. That is My part."

That statement set me free, and the burden lifted. We don't have to "close the deal." We simply are appointed to preach the gospel. At times, you will simply plant a "seed of truth" that will nurture someone along in the journey. I once had the opportunity to share with a young person deeply involved in witchcraft and the occult, who had engaged in demonic supernatural encounters since childhood. In love, I shared a few words of encouragement regarding the hunger for spiritual things and offered an invitation to explore "the higher realms." Pointing in the direction of Christ, I suggested the potential enjoyment of praying to the highest level Spirit in the universe and to ask Him to reveal Himself.

I didn't preach the entire plan of salvation, and neither did I "seal the deal." But in love, I brought the person along one more step in the spiritual search. After being told how much my input was appreciated, she explained that when "preached to" by Christians before, it had been done in an unloving way.

So much so, that it left the impression that no believers cared about unsaved people as individuals.

While interpreting a dream for a psychic once, I had a similar encounter. He was thrilled to hear my interpretation and affirmation of his spiritual sensitivity and hunger. He opened up to a number of our statements about the glory of Jesus, and some very strong seeds ended up being planted. This is an example of the preaching anointing, and every believer is called to this purpose.

The discipleship anointing, however, is different. You are not necessarily called to disciple everyone you lead to the Lord. In fact, sometimes you can't because it is not geographically possible. In chapter 8 of the Book of Acts, Philip was visited by an angel who instructed him to go to a certain destination. As he obeyed the instruction, Philip met an Ethiopian eunuch driving a chariot. The Holy Spirit said, "Go to that chariot and stay near it" (Acts 8:29). Philip preached Jesus to the Ethiopian eunuch within the chariot and, as a result, he came into faith. The apostle then baptized him in water. As soon as they came out of the water, "the Spirit of the Lord suddenly took Philip away, and the [Ethiopian] did not see him again, but went on his way rejoicing" (Acts 8:39). Here, the Holy Spirit ordained a preaching experience for Philip, but then snatched him away before he could engage in any follow-up discipleship. Oh my goodness, Philip didn't even suggest that this brand-new convert attend a church fellowship!

Although caring for new believers is important, we must trust the Holy Spirit to initiate His plan for them. The Spirit that gave the revelation unto salvation is the same Spirit who will lead them on to discipleship. Remember that Jesus is the Author and Finisher of our faith (see Heb. 12:2), not us, a pastor, or even a local church fellowship. The Holy Spirit can use any person and any means to disciple a person. If we rely on Him, we will find rest in this issue. As I have the blessing of serving as a prophetic teacher in the Body of Christ, I am personally involved in a great deal of discipleship. I also engage in lots of evangelism, but I don't always engage in both anointings at the same time.

Should the Spirit lead, we can always be ready to minister in discipleship, but I don't believe that it should be assumed. At times, I spent months discipling a new believer and even brought the person off the street into our home. But even with all that attention and follow-up, the individual did not choose to walk closely with the Lord. On the other hand, I have led people to the Lord and then did not see them for years. One such person approached me at a meeting and reminded me how, a few years earlier, I led them to the Lord on the street. The person had been following God ever since, yet I had completely forgotten the experience. God did a great job of follow-up!

Sometimes, you will simply plant a seed and another will water it. In 1985, we were teaching a group of young people how to engage in street evangelism. These youngsters ended up witnessing to some fellows who had come into town to pick some hallucinogenic "magic mushrooms." The youth preached the gospel to them and one (out of a group of three) prayed the Sinner's Prayer. The trio was leaving town right away, so we prayed for them and off they went. We had introduced ourselves by name, and that was about the extent of it.

Within the next 12 hours, my husband and I received an emergency telephone call at around two in the morning. These guys were beside themselves and had called information for our phone number. Apparently, they had been picked up hitchhiking by three different cars, all of which were driven by Christians. Each driver immediately shared the Lord with them—the message was getting through loud and strong. All of them seemed quite shocked by these "coincidences." Before midnight, they made it into a community a few hundred miles away to visit with a relative. While telling her about the "divine appointments," a demonic visitation arose that freaked them out—thus came their call for help and prayer amidst all this frantic frenzy.

We prayed for the two young men who had not received Christ and the female relative. We also rebuked the demonic attack in Jesus' name and all of them felt the Lord's presence flood their hearts. The next morning, they were back on the road and full of joy. A number of months later, I heard from the one young man. On his arrival, he found a church in his area and got connected with other Christians who loved the Lord. The Holy Spirit was in control!

Discipleship is meant to be relational and not institutional. With Jesus Himself as our example, we find Him hanging out with the disciples on a daily basis. He taught them as they went about their day-to-day life. Today, I believe that the Lord desires us to move more relationally in the area of discipleship. Home cell groups help tremendously with this process.

Many individuals, however, will never enter a church after getting saved. One summer, I met a transvestite who was very hungry for the Lord, yet very insecure and frightened of rejection. I, personally, didn't know of a church in that area where he (she) would feel safe and able to receive healing and deliverance in an accepting environment. Sad to say, but most Western churches are not safe places for new babes in Christ, especially those who many would look upon as "misfits."

Many come to Christ without having their minds renewed, and enter the Lord's house with all sorts of baggage. Can we love them? Are they safe? What about those steeped in the New Age and witchcraft who desire to discover Christ? What about the Free Masonic businessman who has no understanding of the treacheries and deceptions of his secret society? Are we going to secretly whisper about them as they walk through the door? Will we judge them? Will we fear them? Will we gossip about them? How ready are we for discipleship, Church?

I was impressed with one young lady and her prayer partner who held weekly meetings with the transgender and homosexual community on their turf. When walking with those in darkness, you must be very consecrated and hate the garment of sin. These girls kept their hearts pure and spent hours every week praying for each individual. Though members of this homosexual community did not want to be preached at, they were open to friendship. These young ladies worked hard at making friends, and, not long after, the homosexual community trusted them enough to call on them for help. This process was a long one, but the trust and relationships grew. Every week they met with their *friends* and poured love and truth into them. Their "discipleship venue" was over the phone, on the street corner, at the local gay bar, in a coffee shop or a hotel lobby. Wherever their *friends* were open to building relationship, these ladies would be there for them. At each meeting, the young women poured a little more into the homosexuals' lives and then soaked them in prayers of faith and love.

As a young Christian, I personally received a great deal of input at my workplace. Following my conversion, I spent eight months working at a medical lab. About a third of the staff were committed Christians, so we spoke about God at lunch and coffee breaks. Although not an official discipleship meeting, much discipleship still took place—it was a relational setting and it was glorious!

More and more, I believe, we will find discipleship unfolding through relationship. Many Christians today don't even know their neighbors. Getting to know them is easy, however, if we make the time. Everyone is open to a little encouragement and kindness, and this is often the place where discipleship begins. We will probably find that discipleship flows if we make a conscious effort to get to know our neighbors, our coworkers, children and mothers at the playground, those exercising at our gym, and the new visitors at church. Invite people over to your home or out for a coffee. Making an effort to get to know people is where it all begins.

Resource items such as books, tapes, worship and teachings on CD and DVD, and email directives are great tools for discipleship. Our ministry is very committed to distributing resources for this very reason. The Holy Spirit inspires the authors and speakers and uses the anointed content of the resource to disciple masses of Christians. The earth is being filled with anointed expressions of the heart of God through Christian resources.

The Holy Spirit has many expressions for the discipleship mandate to be released. Understand that we are all anointed for discipleship, and it will flow easily as we follow the Spirit's leading. You can easily step into the anointing to preach the gospel and to disciple believers because "it is God who is at work in you, both to will and to work for His good pleasure" (Phil. 2:13, NAS). If we are filled with the Word and the Spirit, then wisdom will flow from our heart and mouth. Be open to His leading and make disciples. A new baby needs lots of love, affirmation, good food, and practical care. We have freely received His love and instruction, so let's freely give as He directs.

9

CHAPTER

Overcoming Intimidation

SUCH CONFIDENCE AS THIS IS OURS THROUGH CHRIST... (2 CORINTHIANS 3:4).

The thought of launching out in any dimension of evangelism can be very scary for most who have never done any outreach before. I remember our first School of Extreme Prophetic. Stacey Campbell and I had done much prophesying in the Church, but not out on the streets. We now found ourselves leading the troops into what was uncharted territory even for ourselves. We had to fight fear and intimidation. *What if we get there and the prophetic does not flow? How do we approach people? What if we get rejected and persecuted? What if we fail? What will the students think if we set a bad example?* All of these are real fears faced by many people. We have witnessed well-known prophets, very eloquent in the Church, who completely freeze up when out on the streets. Coming out of comfort zones is just plain uncomfortable, even for the best of us.

MY FIRST PREACHING EXPERIENCE

Looking back, I'm convinced that God tricked me into my first ministry/preaching experience. I was hosting a prayer meeting at my home when I received a telephone call from a very panic-stricken First Nations woman who lived in a remote village in the northern region of my province. In a desperate tone, she explained that, along with a small group of believers, she had been planning the very first evangelistic crusade in their village. She anxiously related the situation:

"Over the last few months, we have diligently labored, organized, and raised all the money for this event. The evangelist we invited to speak just canceled today due to illness. We have contacted all the priests and ministers we know, and not one of them is able to replace the speaker at such short notice. We called Mary Goddard [a well-known Christian minister in Canada] who was unavailable. She gave us your number, explaining she had trained you and your friend, Marilyn, on the gifts of the Spirit through some classes in your church. She believed the two of you might be of help to us. Could you come? Could you and Marilyn, please come?"

The woman had made quite a request that certainly caught me off guard. "Well, we will have to pray about it," I explained carefully, "because we have young children at home to care for, and we need to see how our husbands and pastors feel about it."

She responded, "We can only give you a couple of hours to make your decision. We will need you to travel here tomorrow. The meetings begin in two days."

When I hung up the phone, I was in shock, to say the least. Marilyn, who had been one of my prayer partners for years, just happened to be with me. When the call came, my pastor was also in our home to attend the prayer meeting. I asked, "What do you think? They're going to phone back in two hours and if we say, 'Yes,' we will need to leave tomorrow."

He looked at us and emphatically exhorted, "You don't need three dreams and a vision to go preach the gospel. The

Word already tells you to go. Just go and obey the Word!" Our husbands felt the same, so we made arrangements to leave the following day.

We had to arrange for friends to care for our children over the weekend as well as organize meals and other details for our families' needs. I was so busy preparing and packing that I hadn't given too much thought to what we had been asked to do. The next day, when we finally boarded the plane, I said to Marilyn, "Do you realize what we're doing?"

Perplexed, she questioned, "What?"

I responded, "We're going to be evangelists at a crusade. Have you ever been an evangelist at a crusade before?"

"No," Marilyn answered.

I, who unfortunately shared her inexperience, said, "Well, neither have I." Suddenly, terror began to surface. We wanted to plead for the pilot to turn the plane around. Looking at ourselves according to natural vision made us confident of one fact: We did not have the ability to fulfill this mandate.

Amidst our panic, however, the Spirit of God rose up within us. We remembered some teaching on praying in tongues, which is one of the spiritual gifts outlined in First Corinthians 12. We were taught that praying in tongues builds up your most holy faith (see Jude 1:20). It's like charging up your spiritual battery, so to speak. This spiritual exercise prepares you to release the glory and majesty of God. So, right there in the airplane, we started praying in tongues. Desperate to get as much of our battery charged as possible, we prayed fast and furiously. Mind you, we did so at a whisper.

When we arrived at our destination, a trio of lovely First Nations ladies greeted us and then drove us on the three-and-a-half hour trek to their village. "There's a prayer meeting tonight in our community," one of them explained, as our bags were being picked up and put in the trunk. "Would you like to join us? It is a special prayer meeting for the crusade." As intercessors at prayer meetings, we were confident and comfortable. We loved praying, so we excitedly agreed.

Here were our thoughts as we quietly conferred together: *Ah, we can pray in tongues for three and a half hours during this journey to the village. That should majorly charge us up!* So in the car's back seat, the two of us prayed in tongues with fervency of spirit. During our passionate display of heavenly intercession, we noticed that our newfound friends in the front seat were rather "stiff" and had what looked to be a "fear seizure." I thought to myself, *Oh, my goodness. I wonder if they understand what tongues are?* As I pondered that question, the Lord spoke within my heart, "They don't even know who I am." I discovered that the driver had recently been born again, but the other two had no knowledge of salvation. Needless to say, we preached the gospel to them and they were gloriously born again. I thought, *Being called to minister as an evangelist isn't really so hard. We've already led two people to the Lord.*

We shared about being filled with the Holy Spirit and speaking in tongues, and then prayed for them right there in the car. All of them became filled by the Spirit and were instantly released in their heavenly language. Now, *five* of us prayed in tongues on the way to the village. Everyone was getting a really good "battery charge"! The beginning of our very first hour of northern ministry turned out to be extremely exciting.

A couple of hours later, we arrived in a most picturesque village, which was nestled in the woods and completely covered with a fresh blanket of newly fallen snow. We pulled up into the parking lot of a quaint Catholic chapel. Upon entering, we found that the prayer meeting was not the typical type we were accustomed to. We had entered into the village's mid-week, Catholic, liturgical prayer service. Although we did not understand everything that transpired in the prayer time, we joined in where we could and loved the sense of community. As the prayers were finalized, the leader rose to close the session and said, "Oh, by the way, we have the evangelists for the crusade with us."

Being called *evangelists* seemed strange to me—it sounded so official. I whispered to Marilyn, "They have no idea that we're just simple housewives. They actually think we're evangelists."

To my horror, I heard the leader continue to speak, "...and we'd like you to come forward and take the meeting."

I looked at my comrade with astonishment as she simultaneously returned a shocked look. "Have you ever taken a meeting before?" I whispered in a panic.

She replied, "No, not like this."

Marilyn had preached about three times previously, and I had preached once. Organizing that first message had taken me an entire summer, and I actually practiced the sermon in front of the mirror on a daily basis. Even with all that preparation, when I finally delivered the message to a small women's group, I was shaking and trembling with intimidation. Now, we were being asked to "take the meeting." I thought, *What have we gotten ourselves into?*

We intentionally stalled a little out of the hope that we hadn't heard the leader correctly. Within the next moment, the speaker once again exhorted us, "Please, come forward now and take the meeting." With much fear and trepidation, we obeyed.

Marilyn is really short with a tiny frame, and I am fairly tall with a much larger frame—it's quite the contrast. We both stood before the people, stiff with fear, yet smiling nonetheless. We had no idea what to do. The faces of the Native congregation looked so expectant, and yet we felt so inadequate. I, for one, was at a loss for words. But when we have no idea what to do, God is never caught off guard. Praise the Lord! He always offers us what we need for each assignment.

As we stood there speechless, a brilliant thought came to me, *Well, we could greet them. That's what we should do.* So, I said, "Hello, we would like to greet you in the name of Jesus." After what seemed to be a long pause, I caught the next little nudge that came into my mind. "Uh, we also bring you greetings from our husbands; they send their greetings and, also greetings from our pastor. In fact, our entire local church greets you." Unfortunately, I quickly ran out of greetings. My faithful friend politely smiled a frozen grin and nodded mechanically throughout my entire introductory discourse. She was not, however, offering much in the way of additional communication, which would have been extremely helpful at the time.

I panicked with no idea what to do next. At that tense moment, the Lord prompted me, "When you were in the gifts of the Spirit class during these last six months, didn't you just step out in childlike faith and exercise My gifts? Well, think of this as the same environment and just step out in faith and do it."

I thought, *Wow, we'll just do it like our instructor Mary Goddard did and we'll see what happens.*

So, I postured my heart to hear from God, and, immediately, a faint thought came into my mind, *"There's someone here with a headache."* I spoke that out to the crowd and faith was released. I thought, *Wow, I actually received a word of knowledge.* Tickled to receive that simple, little "God thought," I didn't realize how common headaches were in a crowd of people. When you step out in faith, you might not get anything that appears earth-shaking, but a word with profound simplicity can produce fruitful ministry. Inwardly, I was convinced that my word was "over the top." Remarkably, as soon as I declared the first word of knowledge, the next one came, "Oh yes, and there's someone with back pain." I also didn't realize how common back problems were, but God is gracious, I was totally excited about receiving these two words of knowledge. After that, God-thoughts came into my mind like popcorn popping. Marilyn also received many words of knowledge, and then we were truly on a roll.

During our gifts of the Spirit class, Mary invited anyone who related to the words of knowledge to come forward for prayer. We prayed for them and released our faith for miracles. In those meetings, we regularly saw the Lord move powerfully. He always honored faith. Reminiscing on our classes gave me courage to invite people to come forward for ministry. I confidently proclaimed, "God is going to release miracles tonight." Following Mary Goddard's example, I simply stepped out in faith, but I didn't feel any particular flood of anointing or power. To my amazement and delight, a whole slew of people came forward. I announced, "Okay, make a straight line across the front here. We're going to pray in faith for your miracle." Looking at Marilyn, I said, "Why don't you start praying at that end of the line and I'll start here? Then, we'll meet in the middle."

With simple faith, we ministered and, to our astonishment, people fell under the Holy Spirit's power. It seemed as if everyone we prayed for received a touch—it was the "beginner's blessing." The power of God landed on all these people. How exhilarating! When Marilyn and I met in the middle, we were surrounded by bodies that had fallen like dominoes. I naively said, "You know, being an evangelist at a crusade is fun, and it's really not that hard either and this is just the prayer meeting. I can hardly wait for the crusade tomorrow."

That night, we fell asleep within moments of our heads hitting the pillow. Early the next morning, a knock came on the door while we were still in our pajamas. A few people who had been at the meeting excitedly reported, "Everyone in the village heard what God did last night. Many of them were not at the session. They want you to come and pray for them." So all day long, we were escorted from house to house, praying for the sick and sharing the gospel with these hungry people. We prayed for entire households to receive Christ and invited the Holy Spirit to touch them in miraculous ways. We learned so much from being with these precious people.

Marilyn and I felt like real missionary evangelists. We didn't know what we were doing most of the time, but we simply trusted God. In each situation, we asked the Lord what to do and then responded to His directives. God faithfully honored every act of faith; He truly is the God of all encouragement. Flying high with excitement, we continued all day with our "missionary exploits." At four o'clock that afternoon, we were taken to a "speaker's meeting."

I had never been to a speaker's meeting before because I had never been a speaker. Marilyn and I were thinking, *Okay, we're here for the speaker's meeting. What do you do at something like this?* They shared the schedule, and their expectations for the next few days. "Tonight, we have a preacher coming in from another community, so you won't be sharing," explained the facilitator. (Inside, I was happy and relieved, but I tried not to let that show.) "But, tomorrow, we want the two of you to speak on deliverance all day. Please teach our people how to overcome witchcraft because many of them are deeply involved. We want you to cast out their devils. Oh, and we also want you to deliver them from their addictions and suicidal and murderous tendencies."

I had attended a few seminars on deliverance ministry and heard testimonies from preachers who had cast out devils in Jesus' name. However, I had never personally cast out a demon yet. Inside, I panicked, but I heard my voice respond, "Okay, we'll be happy to do that. We'll serve you in any way we can."

Marilyn kicked me under the table and shot me a glare that communicated, *What in the world are you committing us to?* After the meeting, she said, "What did you just do? Have you ever cast out a devil before?"

Honestly, I replied, "Well, no, not yet. But I have a feeling we're going to."

Then, Marilyn inquired of me, "I've never taught on casting out devils. Have you?"

"No," I responded, "but I have a simple plan. Tonight, we will go to the meeting and have fun in the anointing, hanging with the conference attendees, and listening to the guest speaker. At the end of the evening, in our hotel room, we'll look up deliverance Scriptures. We know for sure that Jesus cast out devils. Tomorrow, in our sessions we will read the verses on Jesus' deliverance ministry. We will share some of Mary Goddard's testimonies that she taught in class and some stories of televangelists we've heard [that was because we didn't have any of our own yet]. After we share all the Scriptures and testimonies, we'll invite anyone who thinks they have a devil to come forward. Then we'll step out in faith to cast them out. Let's just give it a try and we'll see what God does."

When serving the Lord, you don't have to perform everything with eloquence and sophistication. God honors simple faith and He adores childlikeness. Take all that performance pressure off your shoulders and just be yourself; so that's what we did. With our newfound friends, we celebrated the Lord's goodness in the large, rustic lodge, complete with fireplace and country-and-western band. We were totally lost in the joy of the environment and completely forgot about the next day's responsibilities.

Following worship, the meeting leader said, "I have an announcement to make. We have some good news and some bad news. I'll give you the bad news first. Tonight's speaker just phoned. His car has broken down on the highway. He will not be able to make the meeting. The good news, however, is that we have two evangelists from the coast with us."

With my mind racing, I thought, *Without a doubt Marilyn was the senior preacher and it was only right that she had the honor of this opportunity.* So I said to her, "The leader means you— you're the evangelist and I'm your intercessor."

Marilyn approached the podium with great apprehension. Even though she did not have a sermon outlined on paper, she did have a wealth of sermons within her heart. For years, Marilyn had diligently studied the Word and prayed for several hours a day. If you walk with the Lord daily, studying His Word and meditating on His promises, you will always be ready when called upon. What goes in always comes out. When Marilyn stood up to preach, she was nearly obscured behind a large, carved lectern—only her head was visible. She pleaded silently to herself, *What do I do? I don't know what to say. I don't have a sermon.*

The Lord answered her, "Remember the Kleenex box demonstration!" We had received this training in our prophetic class: When you pull up a tissue, the next one comes up, followed by the next one, and so on. In similar manner, we were trained to believe God for prophetic words one phrase at a time. It's a real step of faith trusting God to give you the next word or phrase as you are delivering the first one. The Lord instructed Marilyn, "You are now going to preach that way, one phrase at a time." She went for it, and I tell you, she preached the most amazing sermon. More than 60 people were born again and over 100 people got filled with the Holy Spirit. Not a bad response for our first night as evangelists at a crusade.

We stayed up into the wee hours of the morning to study our teaching on deliverance. The next day, God was with us as we shared in our very inexperienced manner. We invited any who thought they might need deliverance to come forward; we truly believed that would happen. They flocked to the altar and, in a very simple fashion, we addressed the evil spirits in Jesus' name and demanded that they leave. Suddenly, people started screaming, shaking, convulsing, and trembling under the Holy Spirit's power as God delivered them from bondage. The name of Jesus truly works! He was faithful to His Word. Seeing these dear people touched with His love, freedom, and liberty was awesome! A village witch doctor attended the crusade with a plan to curse us. Instead, he became saved, filled with the Spirit, and delivered. Following his conversion, he burned all his witchcraft paraphernalia.

Good news travels fast. We obtained an unexpected reputation for being deliverance ministers. Testimonies from our crusade spread to many other villages. Invitation after invitation followed, and we often traveled to the remote northern regions of our province. We even had the privilege of traveling by boat through the rapids into isolated regions. Our families came with us on many occasions.

We learned so much during those years. We had wonderful experiences in the native culture, such as cooking banik over an open fire, drying fish, making Indian cream from soap berries, hunting for moose, and catching salmon. The First Nations people were hospitable, extremely generous, loving, and very hungry to know the power and love of Jesus. They had a rich sensitivity of spirit that awakened to the truth found in Christ. Many were easily saved, delivered, and healed. We witnessed numerous miracles, signs, and wonders. Every time we trusted Him to touch lives, God came in power. Walking with Linda Prince during those times was a very special privilege. She is a dynamite apostolic woman of God, who has been a voice for her people for many years. Linda gave us many profound teachings and insights, and I am forever grateful for the opportunity to serve with her.

In one remote village, we saw the majority of one community come to know Christ as Savior. During some special meetings, we witnessed many people receive supernatural deliverance from alcoholism, murderous spirits, and witchcraft. A few years later, I saw two First Nations ministers interviewed on a popular Christian TV program. When the host asked, "How did you get saved?" They replied, "These two crazy women preached the gospel in our village. We were powerfully touched by the Lord and delivered from alcoholism." In listening to their story, I realized that these preachers had been saved during our meeting to their remote village. Now, these two men were out on the frontlines all across the nation for God's Kingdom.

Overcoming the Fear Monster

Each of you has so much potential, but the greatest opposition to releasing your God-given gifts is usually fear and intimidation. The fear of failure and rejection hold many back from fulfilling destiny. Forging into new areas will surely bring us a few stumbles along the way; that is part of our growth process. But we can allow those failures to either be stumbling blocks or stepping stones—it all depends on perspective. Unless you step out in faith, you will never know the anointing within you, let alone allow it to develop and grow.

A child doesn't learn to walk *well* until he begins to walk. I remember when our grandson was attempting to take his first steps. He walked at an early age. He was falling all over the place, but he was determined to overcome. The more he attempted to take steps, the more stable his walking became. By nine months of age, he was going for it. Although he shed a few tears during the process, he kept going. Now, he walks really well and always will. When a child falls during the learning process, do parents get upset with their little one? Of course not! You don't hear them saying, "What's with you anyway? If you can't walk without a mistake, then don't bother trying." No, you hear them cheering on their little guy and encouraging him to take more steps. That is how your Heavenly Father responds when He sees you taking steps to serve Him.

Don't be afraid of failure and the unknown. As an over-comer, you can look fear right in the face and challenge it as you move forward to fulfill the Great Commission. Embrace every opportunity put before you by the Holy Spirit as that is what will unlock your potential. God has greatness waiting for you. He is inviting you to join Him in the greatest adventure of your life. He is inviting you to take light into the darkness. Why don't you go for it!

> *Such confidence as this is ours through Christ before God. Not that we are competent in ourselves to claim anything for ourselves, but our competence comes from God. He has made us competent as ministers of a new covenant... (2 Corinthians 3:4-6).*

10

CHAPTER

God's Media Army

THE ARMIES OF HEAVEN WERE FOLLOWING
HIM, RIDING ON WHITE HORSES AND
DRESSED IN FINE LINEN, WHITE AND CLEAN
(REVELATION 19:14).

In a natural war, the nation that conquers the air space has the greatest tactical advantage. In September 2004, I received an alarming dream in regards to a media army taking its position in this way. I saw God raising up a powerful media army, and many of its troops were young people. Also, apostles, prophets, evangelists, teachers, and pastors had changed roles so as to serve God in the media. This infantry also consisted of screenwriters, filmmakers, radio broadcasters, television producers, cameramen, editors, web media personnel, actors, actresses, and many others. All of them had come together to establish a critical and strategic position to conquer air space for the Lord.

Then, I saw a demonic media army raised up by the enemy to battle against this emerging, holy combatant force. In the dream, a council meeting in the second heaven led satan to dispatch his media army meant to thwart those

Christians contending for the airwaves. Ephesians 2:1-2 states, "As for you, you were dead in your transgressions and sins, in which you used to live when you followed the ways of this world and of the ruler of the kingdom of the air, the spirit who is now at work in those who are disobedient." Attempting to claim its position in the airwaves is a demonic prince that desires to plague the nations with sinful darkness. The Lord, however, is raising up a mighty moving force to establish Kingdom authority in the airwaves. Responding to the media call in this hour is absolutely critical. We must win the battle!

OUR CALL INTO MEDIA

One evening in January 2003, I turned on the TV and it struck me that an unusual number of programs featuring New Age prophets, spirit mediums, psychics, and others operating in supernatural phenomena had flooded the programming options. One false prophet after another displayed "magic" and "spiritual gifts." Such displays vexed my soul. I thought to myself, *Lord where is the true prophetic in the midst of this counterfeit uprising? Where is Your voice, Father? Where is the prophetic Church on the airwaves?*

Secular media often dictates our culture's values. What is on the airwaves conditions the public's mind-set. The media's magnetism is one reason why the darkness of immorality gets so widespread. Every single day, nearly every TV show, movie, and magazine somehow communicates that immorality and anti-Christian values are normal. The media has influenced us to believe that we should want what it puts on display. Much of the degradation, violence, rebellion, and perversity that our society struggles with results from the pervasive weight of the media's corrupted voice.

THE AIRWAVES
BELONG TO THE LORD

God owns everything and we are to steward what He owns, and that includes the airwaves. When the Church abdicates its God-appointed position, our rightful place gets usurped and the airwaves are filled with unhealthy influences. It's not enough for us to complain about all the corruption and immorality on the air, or to simply turn off the TV in frustration; we must take our position back.

That evening in January 2003, the Lord convicted my heart to take personal responsibility for what so grieved me. He asked me if I would be willing to move forward in faith to raise a true prophetic standard amidst the counterfeit uprising. The position abdicated by the Church must be reclaimed. Was I willing to do something about it? Over the years, He has called many others. As a result of those faithful pioneers taking their places, a degree of Christian presence exists on today's airwaves. Much of today's Truth-based programming, however, is hidden inside of Christian networks and primarily structured around church services. All of this, of course, is valuable and possibly God-ordained, but what about the un-churched and the unsaved? How do we address the spiritually hungry who can't relate to how our messages are packaged in services? That evening, the Lord issued a personal challenge to me: "Would you take responsibility to do your part?"

I wondered to myself, *Is there a way we could relate more to all those lost souls who are searching and wanting something to fill the spiritual void, but are not interested in 'church culture'? Was there a way to bring the Father's true prophetic to the spiritually hungry to give them a revelation of Christ?* Bursting into prayer, I asked God to raise up the prophets He had prepared for such a task. That's when the Holy Spirit asked me, "Will you be part of the media army I am raising up? Will you go for Me?" My immediate response was, "No!"

I shared with the Holy Spirit all the reasons why I was a poor choice: I had no training in production; I never had any desire to be on TV; I had no money; and I had no team with any media experience. However, I did promise Him that I would fervently pray for others to be raised up. That was when the Holy Spirit said, "Since when has your lack of ability, income, or team and resources been an issue?"

Right then, I told the Lord I would do whatever He wanted me to, and I would trust Him if He wanted me to produce a television program. "But," I added, "You're going to have to help me, because I don't have a clue where to begin."

EXTREME PROPHETIC TELEVISION

I felt the Holy Spirit say, "Take this up as a prophetic mandate." He then gave me the strategy: Produce a program called *Extreme Prophetic* that would be filmed right in Hollywood, the birthplace of most programming that dictates many of the images and mind-sets of society. The Lord said, "Go right to the jugular of the Babylonian system of the entertainment industry." In the Bible, the Babylonian system speaks of seduction, man's agenda, pride, and a worldly love of money. In other words, it's all about man's name and fame. Seductive evil spirits, such as Jezebel and Leviathan, lurk around the Babylonian kingdom seeking to destroy lives. Hollywood is controlled and influenced significantly by these two dark spirits. Over the years, many Christians have faithfully stood in the gap to dismantle this evil grip over the entertainment industry. As a result of their persevering faith, the Babylonian strongholds *are* coming down! Ministry gatherings like "The Call: Hollywood" and other organized intercessory events and groups have literally broken ground and prepared the way.

The Lord required us to film in Hollywood and to put a stake in the ground that declared, "God's prophetic Church is here!" We were then directed to air the show in Las Vegas, a sin capital of the entertainment industry. The goal of this mandate was to raise up a prophetic intercessory standard against the Babylonian system with its false claim on that territory. At the same time, many other Christians were receiving similar mandates. Others had been forerunners in this area for many years previously. This call to broadcast was a prophetic, intercessory act. I thought it would be used to initiate increased prayer for the airwaves and to call forth more seasoned prophets to step up to the plate. Honestly, I didn't feel called to engage in any more production other than this one assignment. But even at that, I had no idea how to begin. I had the vision, but no clue how to do it. So I prayed for *help!!*

A couple of weeks later, I was speaking at a prophetic conference at Bill Johnson's church in Redding, California. During a break, a woman approached me and explained that she almost never attended Christian conferences and had never before approached a speaker. But the Holy Spirit told her to introduce herself to me. Her name was Shirley Ross and she had spent over 20 years in Hollywood working as a producer. She simply said that she believed that God wanted her to help me somehow. I thought, *Thank You, Jesus.*

I took Shirley to dinner and shared the vision God had given me for *Extreme Prophetic*. Right there, she offered to volunteer time to help put the production together. Now all we had to do was create the show. We had no money to work with, but Shirley managed to corral some volunteers; in six weeks, she put the whole shoot together for a fraction of what such a production would usually cost. God miraculously provided all the finances. In addition, over 300 intercessors signed up to pray daily for the program—it was just amazing!

In our first *Extreme Prophetic* production, Wesley and Stacey Campbell, Larry Randolph, Todd Bentley, and I went to Hollywood to be the guest prophets. Each prophet paid his or her own way and sowed time into the project. Filming was hilarious. Todd and Wesley were as natural as ever, but the cameras totally freaked out Stacey, Larry, and I, and all of us had pasted-on smiles. The make-up artist made us up like porcelain dolls and we didn't feel at all ourselves; this turned out to be a totally different environment than what we were used to.

After filming in Hollywood, we purchased air time in Las Vegas on Warner Brothers Network and were placed between two popular New Age programs. The moment we booked our time, one of the New Age shows—which was hosted by a well-known spirit medium—canceled out. So, we took their slot. What a powerful prophetic statement: The Church was taking back ground! We aired our *Extreme Prophetic* programs for five weeks.

Fruit came immediately. One particular encouraging e-mail was written by an obvious sinner, as evidenced by swear words throughout the note. This man had been powerfully touched by the program and wanted to express his gratefulness. In addition to that, masses of believers seemed to be getting stirred up about taking true prophecy to the airwaves. We received tremendous affirmations from credible, well-known prophets and leaders in the Body of Christ. God's vision for bringing His true prophetic into public visibility through the airwaves was spreading like wildfire.

After successfully shooting and airing our programs, I thought we were finished with the assignment. But the Lord had a different plan: He confirmed that He wanted us to produce a weekly program. At that time, I had a more-than-full-time schedule as an itinerant speaker and ministry leader. I didn't know how I could possibly add in the production of a weekly program, but God had shown time and time again that He knew what He was doing, even if I didn't. So I agreed to continue as did Shirley, who literally laid down her career to honor the Lord's call and serve the program. We had no money, no equipment, no staff, and no talent. But we did have the Lord, and He is always more than enough.

Every step of the way, we followed the Holy Spirit. Quite literally, He was our director. In one visitation, He told us that the program would appear, at first, as if wrapped in swaddling clothes. Our beginnings, like those of Christ, would be humble. But if we followed Him, He promised to cause us to influence people for His glory. God showed up every step of the way. He provided us with two cameras, microphones, a small lighting package, and an editing computer and program. Everywhere we went, He bathed us in favor. Individuals and organizations offered to help, a glorious team of intercessors was raised up, and we received our first financial partners. He was creating the *Extreme Prophetic* family. We had so much fun being completely reliant on the Holy Spirit.

When shooting began on our weekly program, we couldn't afford the exorbitant sum to rent a studio. Instead, we shot in Shirley's condo as we sat at her kitchen table against a wall! We wanted our program to look different from shows that featured preachers behind pulpits or on staged sets. Well, that do-it-yourself, in the home "soundstage" certainly felt different from that! We had never worked a camera, set up lights, or done editing. All we knew to do was ask God for help and read the manuals. To finish shows, we often worked over 18 hours a day and 7 days a week. Many of our initial programs are now embarrassing to look at because of poor lighting, shaky camera, bad sound, and weak transitions. But the Spirit's anointing was powerful and more than made up for our technical inexperience.

The Lord's faithfulness and favor kept showing up, and so did the kindness and blessings of visionaries like Dr. Dick and Joan Dewert and Brad Lockhart at the Miracle Channel in Canada. When we presented our program, they discerned its anointing and potential. Looking past the technical weaknesses, they took a chance on airing us, and did so during prime-time all across Canada! Being favored like that was an amazing gift!

Through our website (www.extremeprophetic.com) and the Miracle Channel's (www.miraclechannel.ca), we began to stream *Extreme Prophetic* out to the nations. Letters, phone calls, and e-mails came in from all over the world. People from Canada, the United States, Israel, Croatia, Romania, Central America, Africa, Japan, Australia, New Zealand, and every continent wrote to tell how they had been touched by the show. Many people watched every week to see if we had a destiny word from the Lord specifically for them. One of our favorite reports came from a man of Moslem background who wrote us, "When I watched your program I felt mysteriously *drawn* by God. I found myself kneeling down and giving my heart to Jesus Christ." Amen!

Since that time, God has opened up other networks for airing and we have grown in relationship with a company of prophets who desire to bring light into the darkness through the airwaves. The prophetic community has been such a wonderful support. Men and women of God such as Bobby Conner, Paul Keith Davis, Heidi Baker, James Goll, Stacey Campbell, Cindy Jacobs, Graham Cooke, John Paul Jackson, Todd Bentley, and others have given us their blessings as well as personal interview time. Through the Elijah List, my good friend Steve Shultz has since launched a prophetic television network on the web and he interviews prophets carrying profound, critical messages. Thousands of viewers from around the world watch this web TV. Many others, like Wendy and Rory Alec from God TV, are claiming airwaves globally with a fresh prophetic authority.

THE MONEY DEMON

For the most part, secular media is controlled by money. As part of the Babylonian strategy, how much money you have usually determines whether or not you step into any form of media or not. When we began, someone told us not to start unless we had a million dollars. Well, at that point, we didn't even have a million cents. But we proceeded because of the Lord's direction and trusted Him one day at a time. In the beginning, one contract offered us money to produce the program but put controlling interest of *Extreme Prophetic* in the hands of investors. We felt the Lord restrain us from going that route; He made it clear that He wanted to raise up His own financial partners and enlist them as part of His volunteer media army.

When God called us to the media, I had been in public prophetic ministry for over 23 years. I had planted churches, worked in missions, and engaged in apostolic projects, but I had never experienced the financial pressure that I did when stepping into media. The warfare was actually tangible and, at times, the pressure was unbearable. To proceed, we needed more personnel, more sophisticated equipment, and more software than we actually had. Everything came with a huge price tag. If we didn't make the investment, then we couldn't upgrade our quality, which meant not being able to take more air space.

At one point, I remember feeling a heavy weight of demonic assault. I was overseas when I received word from our bookkeeper, who said, "The well is dry." We had no money left in our account and only had two weeks until the month's end to make our budget. I asked Shirley Ross to inform each staff member on the production team of our situation. Ron and I owned a small home that we could sell or mortgage to cover expenses for one month but after that we had nothing left of our own to invest. We could offer them the security of the current month's salary but could not promise anything beyond that. Although we were standing on the truth, we wanted them to know all the facts, should they need to find other employment. Our team members had families to care for and needed provision. We communicated the situation with every worker. After sharing, each individual stated that they were in *Extreme Prophetic* for the long haul; if we had no money for paychecks, they would trust God to meet their needs, even if that meant taking a second job.

DAVID'S MIGHTY MEN

Just months before, these people had given up their secure employment positions and laid down businesses so as to pursue God's call on their lives. Now, they were being severely tested. I was reminded of David's mighty men (see 1 Chron. 11:10-19) who were willing to risk their well-being, and even their lives, to defend a field for their King. Our team members had committed to taking the airwaves for God. To see the Kingdom advance, they were willing to work long hours, receive no pay, and fight ferocious warfare. They remained focused and faithful as did our financial partners and intercessors!

We praise the Lord that His provision came through—at the final hour, but it was enough to meet everyone's needs. The testing of these difficult months proved the heart of God's servants. What prevailed was an opposite spirit to the Babylonian mind-sets of greed, self-exaltation, and pride and breakthroughs followed. The Lord promises to always give His people victory in Christ (see 2 Cor. 2:14). As we long as we don't lose faith, God's media army is going to win on every front. God is more than able to give us the territory so that He will be lifted up in the earth.

ANGELIC VISITATION

"Are not all angels ministering spirits sent to serve those who will inherit salvation?" (Heb. 1:14). In our time, many people are receiving angelic visitation—it is one of the earmarks of harvest season. The Book of Acts is full of evidence of angelic assistance during harvest and persecution. If you desire to bring light into the darkness, be confident that angels will be assigned to protect, provide, strengthen, and bring communication to you. God's media army consists not only of those who are called in His Body, but also heavenly hosts who are there to support and encourage us. Increased angelic visitation will occur within the media. I have seen prophetic visions of angels, spiritual winds, and fires showing up on sets and during shoots. Amazing signs and wonders will accompany many of those who are walking with God in media mandates this season.

ARE YOU BEING CALLED?

God's media army is truly being raised up in this hour. Perhaps you are personally being recruited. He is calling intercessors, financial partners, technical and administrative support, creative directors, producers, and all sorts of individuals who are willing to stand for Him. He is looking for those set apart for His purposes, who are not compromised with love for money, fame, and power. He is calling those who love their King and, who like David's mighty men, are willing to defend the airwaves for Him. Gross darkness prevails in and through the airwaves, and the Lord wants His light bearers to invade the darkness. If your heart is beating with a call towards media, then pray for Him to pave the way for you. He is so good and will more than meet you as you step out in faith. Try praying the following prayer:

Dear Heavenly Father,

I commit myself wholly to You in spirit, soul, and body. I make myself available to serve You in any area of the media. I feel called to Your media army and I say "Yes!" All that I am and all that I have is Yours. Thank You, for Your abundant grace that enables me to do all things in Christ who strengthens me. Open the way and I will walk in it. I am ready to serve You by taking Your light into the darkness! In Jesus' name, Amen!

11

CHAPTER

It's All About Him!

In Chapter 2, I shared a vision of a believer who ran into darkness while holding up a torch of Christ's light. As illustrated through that opening vision, the central focus of *Light Belongs in the Darkness* is about carrying the Light Himself into places that do not know Him. In order to carry the Light, we must *know* the Light. It is too easy for us to catch wind of the coming harvest season and—with our own self-efforts—pull together a program of evangelism so as to fulfill prophetic destiny.

The human soul is fully capable of coming up with great ideas and initiating plans of action. Of course, these efforts may potentially produce a measure of fruit, since the Lord will always honor His Word and faith. But what He is actually looking for is a Body who will represent His heart because they know Him and love Him.

The Kingdom is all about relationship. The reason why God sent His Son Jesus to save us was because He desired relationship. Not only *does* He love, but He *is* Love and He desires to express this pure love to and through us. He is calling us to draw near to Him so we will be transformed by His presence and love what He loves. He wants our hearts to be passionate about what He has passion for, and He is passionate over the lost!

When I first became born again, I preached to anyone who would listen. As a result of being so filled with blessings of Christ's life, love, and forgiveness, I wanted the whole world to know Him and share my experience. I loved everyone in a new and refreshing way because I had personally experienced His love. Over time, I engaged in more evangelism, teachings, outreach, and projects until they became a regular part of my daily life. I loved it all! Without being consciously aware of it, however, I became very project-oriented. It came about so subtly that I didn't even notice.

One evening, while listening to Jackie Pulinger from Hong Kong preach a very convicting message, I clearly understood how I had been selfishly engaging in evangelism rather than serving the lost with pure motives. I enjoyed going out soul-winning on the streets, and I felt personally fulfilled while going out with a team. That self-fulfillment, however, had become part of my motivation for engaging in evangelism projects. In some ways, I believe I entered into a measure of pride. When reporting how many souls we led to Christ after an outreach, I often felt a sense of personal satisfaction. In no way am I suggesting that reports of what the Lord accomplishes through His people should be silenced. Not at all! In fact, we need to report all the marvelous things He is doing. But we must make a point of examining the motives of our hearts while doing so.

In those days, we would get "persecuted" on the streets at times. People once in a while would yell out profanities, throw things, and, at times, attempt to chase after us. All this commotion seemed to add to our excitement. After all, we were being persecuted for the sake of righteousness. After listening to Jackie's message that evening, I realized that, for the most part, we probably hadn't been persecuted at all; the lost were simply discerning an impure motive and had reacted as a result.

In response to the conviction, I repented of all my wrong motives and actions. I invited Him to fill me with His heart for the lost. God clearly revealed to me that He was a friend of the sinner and, if I would allow Him, He would reveal His heart. All I had to do was humble myself and draw near to Him. On returning home from that engagement, I scheduled a day to visit the very inner-city streets I had witnessed to in previous years. This time, I found Jesus on the streets and started to feel His heart of love for the lost in deeper ways than I had ever experienced in the past. I walked the streets, looked at the brokenness all around me, and cried out to God, "Let my heart break for them as Yours does." That was a special day in my life. I felt a deeper love for the lost than I had ever known before. That day on the streets, I met the Lord in a special way. The lost are the love of His life and He wants us to share in this love.

The greatest key to doing successful ministry is knowing His heart. He is so willing to reveal Himself to us, but He will not release His deep passion to everyone. He reserves that for those who love Him deeply and will draw close to His heart. The lost are His greatest treasure and He will only share His vulnerability with those who have a deep love for Him. Knowing this intimate place in Him is such an honor and privilege. Everyone who longs to know and love Him with a pure heart is invited to experience it.

Once you are filled with the essence of His love, then it becomes easy to witness for Him. The lost will be drawn to you. They will trust you and will discern Christ's true love within you. Being filled with His love for the lost must be the greatest goal for those who desire to bring in the harvest. This is how we carry the true Light to those in darkness—it is all about Him.

PLUGGED IN

Jesus is the same yesterday, today, and forever! His love for the lost has never diminished. As men's hearts are drawn towards sin and lawlessness, the darkness is becoming increasingly dark. Rebellion and corruption is on the increase in the Western world, and tremendous conflicts between the kingdoms of darkness and light prevail throughout the earth. Amidst all this, we must look to the One who has stood faithful through every wave of man's rebellious uprising throughout history. God has never compromised and has never withdrawn love or faith.

He is Savior, Healer, Deliverer, and King. He is also the only one worthy in all creation to open the seals of judgment that will come upon the earth. He is altogether awesome! He is the Light. He invites us to the fullness of His power and love, and to know Him in fullness so that we might truly represent Him in the dark days ahead. All of this comes through true intimacy and connection with Him. Just as a lamp cannot illuminate a dark room without being plugged into a power source, we cannot light up a dark world without an intimate connection with Him. Intimacy with the Source is the key to brightening the world with His Light.

DISTRACTIONS

For a two-year period, I found myself fighting distractions while worshiping and engaging in devotion times with Christ. Many Christians I discuss this with have also had similar experiences. When I inquired in conferences or some other gatherings of believers, usually between 85 to 100 percent of people have been assaulted in this way. What does the distraction look like? You start to have your devotional time and, suddenly, all sorts of extraneous information fills your mind. You might think, "I need to check my e-mail. I need to go make some coffee. I'll just do this first and then go back to prayer." Before long, the time set apart for fellowship with God is gone and your day has progressed without any time in the secret place.

Man's carnal nature is at enmity against God. The soul often leans more to that which resists Him than to that which draws us close to His heart. In many ways, I find my unruly carnal soul a greater enemy than the devil himself. We serve Him in the deepest, darkest places because He is worthy. Our empowerment to go, however, is birthed out of our intimacy with Him. How can we go into the darkness if we are not abiding in the Light? What follows are some helpful tips to assist you in overcoming distractions to spending time with God:

1. Make a firm commitment to spend time with Him. Set the time into your schedule and commit to it.

2. Set a Bible reading plan for each day. Attempt to read through the Bible at least once each year in a methodical plan. In addition, you can read portions and study the Word as the Holy Spirit directs, but the daily disciplined reading will help you remain focused.

3. Take command over all unruly thoughts. Although it is a grueling process, persistence will bring results. Throughout the day, draw your thoughts onto the Lord.

4. Invite the Holy Spirit to help and empower you to take an aggressive stand to contend for your intimate place in His presence.

5. Make loving Him a priority over all else. As you minister to Him and while soaking in His love, He will fill you with His heart. Then you are ready to run with the vision and will truly shine as a light in the darkness.

12

CHAPTER

If the Arm of God
Has Touched You...

I want to close this book with one of the most impacting prophetic calls to the Body of Christ that I have ever heard. May this word truly cause you to be stirred into action and filled with hope for a dying world.

THE BLOOD

As delivered through Stacey Campbell

And He Himself is the propitiation for our sins, and not for ours only but for those of the whole world (1 John 2:2).

Then He said to Thomas, "Reach here your finger and see My hands and reach here your hand and put it into My side and be not faithless, but believing" (John 20:27).

What the Lord showed me was a vision of the power of the Blood of Christ. He began to speak to my heart of how powerful is the Blood of Christ. It is powerful not only for the sins of the Church, but for the sins of the whole world. For all time, for every last single created human being, that is how powerful is the Blood of Christ.

The Lord said to me, "My Church does not believe in the power of the Blood of Christ." He says that when they see them come up by ones and twos and be converted, then they say, "Oh, because I have seen that, I believe in that." But when they watch TV and read the newspaper, they look upon society with despair and disgust, and do not see it through the eyes of the power of the Blood of Jesus Christ. They do not rise up from reading the newspaper and say, "The Blood of Christ can heal that; the Blood of Christ can redeem that; the Blood of Christ can save that derelict."

They do not get up from the TV and say, "I will go now, because I believe in the power of the Blood of Christ to redeem all mankind—even the homosexual, even the alcoholics, even the prostitutes, even the abused." But they read the newspapers and are filled with despair and they say, "Oh, woe is me; woe is our nation; look what has happened to us."

And the Lord says that He is looking for a people, and He has come to His Church. He has come to visit His Church in much the same way that He went to visit His people Israel. He went to His own; He went to His own first. Why? So that He could commission them to go to the Gentiles.

He has come to His Church. Why? So that He can commission them to go to the world. I believe that the Lord is looking for a people who will rise up and say, "I will go into the darkest part of society. I will go to the prisons. I will go to the streets. I will go out into the world. And I will go and I will say, 'The Blood of Christ can do this; the Blood of Christ can heal the sick; the Blood of Christ can redeem even the deepest, darkest secret sin of all mankind.' "

God says that His Arm is not short that it cannot save. His Arm is not short that it cannot save England. His Arm is not short that it cannot save Canada. His Arm is not short that it cannot save Europe. His Arm is not short that it cannot save Iran. His Arm is not short that it cannot save Thailand. There is nothing, there is no one too far from the Blood of Christ that they cannot be redeemed. But He says, "I come to My own and they go nowhere." I feel as if the Lord is saying one thing, He is saying this: "That if the Arm of God has touched you, hold it out and touch someone else, even if only one."

LIGHT BELONGS IN THE DARKNESS!

YOU ARE LIGHT IN CHRIST!

GO!

resources

EXtreme Prophetic
with Patricia King

RECEIVING THE ANOINTING

The Spirit of the Lord God is upon you!

Are you hungry to move into a greater flow of God's *dunamis* power? This teaching from Patricia King is a message from the Book of Acts full of insights and instructions on how to be filled with the Holy Ghost power that He desires us to walk in. *Receiving the Anointing* is available online at

www.extremeprophetic.com.

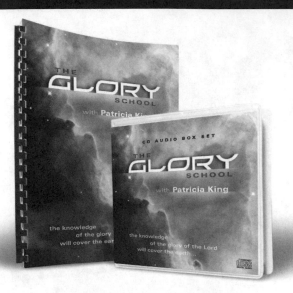